BORN to SERVE

The Story of a Change-Maker!

DR. ERIC EDOKPAIGBE IDEHEN

BORN TO SERVE

Copyright © 2025 Dr. Eric Edokpaigbe Idehen

All rights reserved. No part of this book may be reproduced or transmitted in any form or by any means without the written permission of the author.

Published by:
Eleviv Publishing Group
Centerville, OH 45458
info@elevivpublishing.com
www.elevivpublishing.com

ISBN: 978-1-952744-97-6 (PB)
         978-1-952744-98-3 (HC)
         978-1-952744-91-4 (eBook)

Printed in the United States of America

Table of Contents

Dedication

Foreword

Acknowledgment

Introduction

My Early Childhood... *14*

Education and Early Ambitions... *19*

The Building Block of My Career... *41*

Building a Family... *70*

Founding the Nonprofit: The Birth of Cornerstone of Hope Orphanage... *90*

My Personal Philosophy and Leadership Style... *114*

Major Achievements and Legacy... *121*

Trials and Resilience: Shaped by Adversity... *127*

Reflections on Turning 60... *133*

Afterword: A Message to Readers... *140*

Appendix

DEDICATION

This book is dedicated to the kids of Cornerstone of Hope Orphanage (Nigeria), all orphans worldwide, and the Late Gabriel Edokpaigbe Idehen's family.

FOREWARD

It is with great honor that I pen this foreword for the remarkable journey chronicled in this book by my brother, Dr. Eric Idehen. As the eldest sibling in our family, Eric and I have shared countless experiences in Nigeria and abroad, which have given me a unique perspective on his extraordinary life. His unwavering commitment to making a positive difference in the lives of others stands out as a testament to his character, especially in our increasingly self-centered world. Eric's journey has not been without its challenges; however, these trials only underscore his dedication to selfless service.

His passion for nurturing relationships is evident, as illustrated by the enduring bonds he maintains with his childhood friends, a theme that is woven throughout this narrative. This book does not merely recount events; it embodies Eric's genuine love for humanity and his desire to inspire others. In sharing his life story, Eric invites us to reflect on the profound impact of kindness and community. It is a privilege to witness his journey and to share his insights with you, the reader. This book will undoubtedly inspire you as it has inspired me.

In the tapestry of life, it is often the small and ordinary actions that weave the most profound differences. Eric exemplifies this truth through his unwavering passion for serving others. He reminds us that the little we have when shared generously can create ripples of kindness that transform not only our lives but also the world around us. Rather than waiting for the perfect moment, Eric makes time to engage in small acts of love, embodying the belief that both the minor and significant aspects of life hold the potential for profound and lasting change.

The journey of the Cornerstone of Hope Orphanage stands as a testament to this philosophy. Over the past two decades, Eric has played a pivotal role in transforming the lives of more than 150 orphans in Nigeria. His commitment illustrates that monumental achievements often result from countless small gestures infused with great love. Eric's dedication to community service has inspired me to embrace a similar path.

His example motivates me to give back through volunteering and infuses my professional endeavors with a spirit of generosity. This book captures not only Eric's journey but also the essence of how small, heartfelt actions can lead to extraordinary outcomes. In this compelling work, Eric draws upon his extensive professional and personal experiences to offer profound reflections that resonate deeply with readers.

As a psychologist, he embodies a unique blend of ethical insight and a commitment to social change, driven by a selfless passion to make a meaningful impact, even in small but consistent ways. Throughout the pages of this book,

Eric shares his life journey—a narrative enriched not only by his dedication to serving others but also by his academic and professional accomplishments. His insights illuminate the transformative power of small actions, demonstrating how they can lead to significant change in our lives and communities. Engaging with this book will enhance your understanding of the often-overlooked beauty of self-reflection.

While it can be daunting to explore our own stories, Eric provides a guiding light, making the process accessible and enriching. We all have narratives that deserve to be told, and this book serves as a valuable tool for those seeking to uncover and share their journeys. In our journey through life, Eric and I have often found ourselves reflecting on our shared experiences and challenges, particularly our commitment to serving others.

The joy of giving surpasses the pleasure of receiving. For over two decades, Eric has jokingly suggested writing a book to inspire those around him with lessons from his life journey. Throughout this time, I have encouraged him to document his experiences chronologically, recognizing the potential impact his story could have.

At long last, in 2025, Eric unveiled this remarkable book. It is a treasure trove of rich life experiences and profound testimonies that resonate deeply with many of our encounters. This work broadens our understanding of ourselves and invites us to embark on a journey of self-discovery.

The insights shared within these pages nourish the spirit and ignite the spark of our undiscovered vocational callings, guiding us toward the signs that encourage us to act. Everyone is born with a unique mission, yet uncovering it can often be a challenging task. This is where Eric's book becomes an invaluable resource—a beacon of guidance for those seeking to understand their true selves.

Through his exemplification of the joy found in giving and serving others, Eric offers a powerful testament to the transformative nature of humanity. As you delve into this book, may you find inspiration and direction on your path of discovery.

Sincerely,
Dr. Eghosa Edo Idehen, DBA, PhD.

ACKNOWLEDGMENT

Writing this book has been thrilling, and I am eternally grateful to those who supported me along the way. I am eternally grateful to my family for their ongoing love, patience, and support during the many hours I spent writing this book. Your belief in me inspired me to keep going.

To my editor, Vivian Elebiyo-Okojie, your incisive observations, proofreading of drafts, and meticulous critiques have significantly enhanced this manuscript, making it far superior to what I could have achieved independently. I thank you for your dedication, care, and choice of words.

To my brother, Dr. Eghosa Edo Fred Idehen, thank you for being my sounding board, writing the book's foreword, and offering candid critiques and boundless motivation. Your support has been invaluable.

I would like to extend my thanks to Pastor Richard Webb, under whose leadership and guidance I embarked on this project. Your instruction has been a blessing, and I owe my greatest gratitude to the words you've shared.

To my mentor, Pastor Jeremy Johnson, Lead Pastor of Outreach Lutheran Church of Hope, I would like to offer the deepest and sincerest gratitude for his enduring spiritual guidance and vision. His support has helped me cope with stress with guidance and meet frustration and challenges with determination and purpose. He is a strong pillar, unshakeable yet humble, powerful in a quiet yet firm way, and an excellent role model. I admire his leadership style immensely. Throughout my job search, he stood by me every step of the way, reminding me that God's timing is not our own. Thanks for your valuable guidance and punctuality; they are greatly appreciated.

Finally, to the reader: Thanks for reading this book. Stories live and breathe because of you; I am honored to share this with you.

With gratitude,
Dr. Eric Edokpaigbe Idehen

INTRODUCTION

This book is a tribute to the power of sincerity, trust, determination, and faith. For the past sixty years, I have gained lessons that will encourage and empower you, the reader, to find your balance, purpose, and strength. My life is one of humility, resilience, and a steadfast faith in the power of real connections and unselfish giving.

I learned the importance of trust at an early age. Other people trusted me without a doubt whenever I gave a word as a child. That sense of reliability molded my character in my childhood. Keeping my word, showing up early for commitments, and standing by what I said have become habits for me. Trust, I've learned, forms bonds of strength that have worked in my favor both personally and professionally.

Life also taught me to accept both evil and good. I prefer to think of myself as "tea without sugar," capable of savoring the clean taste of life without combinations. Having had little during childhood, I became accustomed to satisfaction and steadiness. Such a disposition has been my strong pillar, enabling me to remain calm in times of hardship. I would like readers of this book to discover their own "aha" moments, to understand why they have struggled through some of the things they have, and to emerge stronger for it.

At its core, this book is about compassion. Genuine kindness isn't about recognition; it's about doing what's right, even when no one is watching. I've always believed in a simple mantra: *Do Something Good (DSG)* daily. This habit of small, positive actions has been my antidote to negativity and has helped me build a life filled with purpose and optimism.

Depression and desperation were never options for me. I hope my story encourages individuals experiencing difficult times to see the light at the end of their tunnels. Whether you grew up poor, experienced setbacks, or faced numerous failures, I hope this book inspires you. My journey shows that falling doesn't define the person; rising does.

Faith is another cornerstone of my journey. Often, we forget that what we have today is what we once prayed for. I want readers to reflect on their faith journeys, recognize how far they've come, and appreciate the blessings they might have overlooked. I grew up with nothing; when I say nothing, I mean I didn't grow up with abundance. I want people, whoever is reading my book, to be able to find that balance.

This book also explores my career and the challenges I faced as someone who migrated from a small town to a larger city and eventually to the diaspora. Like life itself, career success is about perseverance and the willingness to start over when necessary. I stand before you today because of the many people who have helped me along the way. It truly does take a village, and I draw upon the African philosophy of Ubuntu: "I am because we are." This interdependence has been critical to my happiness and success.

Finally, this book is the epitome of generosity. Generosity is not necessarily dependent on material possessions, but rather an act that stems from a position of genuine compassion, regardless of one's possessions. I have realized that giving benefits the recipient and profoundly affects the giver. I have experienced this through my work at the Orphanage and acts of kindness to strangers. Selfless giving creates a bountiful harvest of peace and contentment.

In my story, I hope that you find inspiration to meet life's challenges with dignity, choose authenticity, and make selfless contributions. In whatever town or city you read these words, you will find something in here for yourself: a hard-won lesson, a spark of hope, or the assurance that no matter where you find yourself on this earth, you are never alone.

This book is a testament to the sacrifices and the lessons of my childhood. It is a tale of the power of learning, the power of family, and the power of endurance in the face of life's adversities and trials. In these, I learned that one measures not in dollars and cents, but in one's ability to withstand, give selflessly, and remain principled, standing by one's values.

MY EARLY CHILDHOOD

I was born on May 19, 1965, to the family of Mr. Gabriel Edokpaigbe Idehen and Mrs. Theresa Osayawe Idehen (née Eguavoen). My father hails from Ikhuen, and my mother hails from Igbuobazuwa in the Ovia Local Government Area of Edo State, Nigeria. My parents' union was that of an educated pair

My father was a school teacher, and my mother's father, my grandfather, was a headmaster. My parents met when my father was re-posted to Igbuobazuwa, where my mother was still in teachers' training college. They married, and my father's job later moved them to Wkehuan Village in the Orhionmwon Local Government Area, where I was born.

As the firstborn, I became a part of a story defined by movement, resilience, and the pursuit of better opportunities. My earliest memories were formed in the teachers' quarters of schools where my father taught. My mother, a stay-at-home mom during those years, supplemented our meager income by frying akara (bean cakes) and donuts, which she sold to support the family.

My father was a disciplinarian. He was strict and fussy, like a headmaster, and always presented himself as "Mr. Perfect." He brought his high standards to our household as well, where he insisted that I, being the eldest, set a model for my siblings. He was particularly tough on me; I knew my younger brothers and sisters would follow in my footsteps if I could get it right.

This expectation left little room for mistakes, as errors often came with harsh consequences and the fear of ridicule. I worked hard to meet his standards, avoiding anything that could be perceived as a misstep. I remember my childhood days in our compound, where mangoes, guavas, and others were grown. The trees gave us play and food, especially during the rainy season when the wind would dislodge the ripe fruits. My siblings and I loved to run out to harvest them before the rain could get us wet.

There was a particular day whose memories remain vivid in my mind. It was just starting to rain, and the wind was already shaking the leaves off the trees. My mother had brought my younger siblings inside, but I ran outside to get mangoes. When I was standing under the tree, a lightning bolt struck. It was like a burning arrow tore through the tree and touched the ground near me.

It was frightening but fascinating. I stood still, unable to make sense of what I had just witnessed until I heard the frantic cries of my mother. She rushed outside, scooped me up, and pulled me inside. I was unable to explain what had happened. I have seen fire," I told her, "but I don't know what it was. I did not even know the word "lightning." The sight left an impression on me that lasted, and the vivid picture of that explosion of flame haunted my imagination for years.

Even when I was grown, and I knew what lightning was, the memory seemed almost mythical, a reminder of nature's power that was chastening. At the time, I sensed that the world beyond our compound was more complicated than what I was familiar with. Despite my parents' efforts to isolate us from the truth, I would occasionally overhear them mentioning war and battles.

The whispers spoke to me of more pervasive tension, but they never let it interfere with the security and stability they fought to achieve in our lives. In retrospect, I can appreciate how much they protected us, even when the world was so insecure. My father anticipated my actions, being the oldest, to set an example for my other siblings. He held me to a very high level, demanding perfection in my studies, behavior, and discipline.

My parents never tolerated mistakes lightly, and my adolescence was spent struggling with the dual responsibility of learning quickly and not disappointing those around me. At the age of five, the reality of the Nigerian Civil War began to seep into my consciousness. As my parents shielded us from the realities, I recall running out with toys and personal items to escape to Benin City. On the trip, I witnessed men carrying guns, homeless people, and the unspoken fear that surrounded my family. While confusing at the time, those experiences taught me the importance of survival, resilience, and family unity.

In Benin City, we moved into a bustling family house on Aruosa Street, a place teeming with relatives, noise, and chaos, characteristic of large, extended families. This stark contrast to the quieter life we had lived in the teacher's quarters also introduced me to a broader circle of cousins and the lessons that come with sharing space and resources.

My education began at St. Joseph Primary School, which later became Uwa Primary School. Study was the hallmark of our home life. My father, who was always a teacher, made us study more than our peers, giving us homework that we would receive in school before it was taught. As the headmaster's son, my grades and behavior had to be immaculate. The discipline was stringent, but it instilled an unwavering respect for study and discipline.

Our days were dominated by scarcity, creativity, and determination. We had no playthings; we created games and toys with wooden odds and ends, buttons, and scraps. We built pushcarts, played strategy games like Ludo and Ogirise, and invented games that required precision and well-stretched imagination. We also enjoyed these, and they helped stimulate our development of skills to solve puzzles and improvise, skills that have proven valuable to me since entering adulthood.

By high school age, I was aware of our poverty at Adolor College, Benin City, Ugbowo. I knew I was poorer than most of my classmates because of my clothing and lack of luxuries. I was humiliated for wearing traditional African attire to a social event where jeans and sneakers were the norm, which pushed me to excel. These experiences also instilled in me the value of hard work and persistence.

I worked odd jobs, saved to buy my belongings, and vowed a better life for myself and future family members. Growing up in a strict and loving household taught me discipline, hard work, tenacity, and honesty. My parents' strictures, though at times too severe, held us in line and beyond the grasp of the negative elements in the external environment. My mother taught us the value of hard work, self-reliance, and sympathy. Together, they taught us survival skills and the know-how to keep our heads above water and endure in the midst of adversity.

EDUCATION AND EARLY AMBITIONS

Education constituted the foundation of my upbringing, a heritage from my father, a teacher who had faith in the liberating value of education. I started at a modest primary school, moving to yet another (Edaiken Primary School), from which I graduated in 1977. Looking back, my finest subject during those formative years was arithmetic. Its logic and solution-based nature captivated me, and I was consistently good at it. English, as one of the core subjects, was slightly more challenging, but having my father around meant that I couldn't give up on it.

At 12, I went to Adolor College, a high school that served as a stepping stone to our bigger aspirations. I was one of the younger students in my year group, a status that presented both problems and opportunities. While some of my classmates were significantly older, even full-grown adults with beards, I quickly learned that education was not about size or age but about discipline, focus, and the capacity to absorb and apply knowledge.

From a young age, I wanted to become a pilot. Airplanes fascinated me, and I often looked up at the sky, captivated by their movement and imagining what it would be like to control such a magnificent machine. That dream was my beacon. When I discovered that excelling in sciences was a prerequisite for becoming a pilot, I committed myself to pursuing science subjects. This decision became the defining focus of my academic life.

SOWING THE SEEDS OF LIFELONG LEARNING

My dad's work as a teacher set the course of my studies and attitude toward education. My dad believed strongly in the benefits of academic learning, even during the holidays. While other children were playing outside, my siblings and I attended "lessons" or participated in summer lectures held at schools in our neighborhood.

The courses kept us studying year-round, reviewing subjects learned in the previous term and covering new material to be studied in the upcoming term. At the time, I did not appreciate the discipline of the routine, but looking back, I see how these lectures instilled in me the passion and discipline of learning, a habit that persisted throughout the rest of my life.

I was fortunate to have a circle of friends who shared my commitment to academic excellence. All of them are highly successful now: Minister Osula, Mike Odion Isiramen, Napoleon Omomila, and Osaretin Osaige. They were more than just classmates; they were partners in ambition. We were not from wealthy homes, but we were determined to succeed and rise above the hand we'd been dealt. Together, we formed a support system, challenging and competing in a spirit of camaraderie. Our collective focus on the sciences helped us grow academically.

Despite my enthusiasm for science, I struggled with art subjects, particularly English language, which was a problem when I graduated from Adolor College. To pursue higher education, I needed a credit in English Language, which I lacked. My father's aspirations for me to study medicine or pharmacy were dashed, and I felt a deep sense of disappointment, both for myself and for him.

However, setbacks often lead to new opportunities. Once I could not pursue a career in medicine or pharmacy, I decided to study Quantity Surveying; its blend of mathematics, architecture, and practical application in managing construction economics and technology intrigued me. So, in 1983, I enrolled at Auchi Polytechnic to study this discipline. Enrolling at Auchi Polytechnic was a transformative experience.

As the first in my family to attend higher education, I carried the weight of my family's expectations. My father, in particular, viewed my education as a means to fulfill his dream of seeing his children break the cycle of poverty. Quantity Surveying was a new course at the Polytechnic, taught by expatriates from Glasgow. My department chairperson, Professor Elliot, was a mentor who changed my life. His rigorous and methodical approach to instruction had a profound impact on me. He was a perfectionist and consummate professional, and I aspired to be like that. Years later, even my youngest son was named after him, spelled in the UK fashion of "Elliott."

At the Polytechnic, however, I was freer than I had ever been before. Away from home, my parents could no longer discipline me either. Initially, this newfound independence led to distractions. Social activities and the camaraderie of hostel life often took precedence over academics. However, realizing that my actions would eventually reflect on my family and reach my father kept me grounded.

Boarding school was both challenging and educational. Sharing a living space with students from diverse backgrounds taught me valuable lessons in tolerance, flexibility, and the importance of protecting one's belongings. The hostel became a microcosm of the larger society, where skills in survival, negotiation, and building interpersonal relationships were learned.

While I was at Auchi Polytechnic, I often thought about the immense freedom I had. My dad wasn't there, and my mom wasn't there to watch over me. It felt liberating at first, as if the world was mine to explore. "Oh, party on, let's go. I'll read later," I often thought. While I didn't completely lose my footing, I could feel the impact of my choices. The speed and focus with which I used to study began to slip. Time seemed to shrink as I realized there were only 24 hours a day, and I was trying to do too much. Polytechnic life brought its unique challenges. Growing up in a hostel, away from the comfort and familiarity of home, I found myself navigating new dynamics.

At home, I was used to sharing a room with my siblings. In the hostel, I now had to share space with people from vastly different homes, religions, and walks of life. Adjusting to dorm life wasn't easy. Back then, rooms were often shared between freshmen and seniors. Seniors had the privilege of a single bed, while freshmen had to contend with bunk beds; as it was, I ended up with the bottom bunk.

This setup taught me valuable lessons about coexistence and respect for others. I had to learn how to navigate personalities, accommodate different habits, and ensure harmony in our shared space. It was also where I learned a critical skill: how to protect my belongings. Just because something was left in your room didn't mean it would still be there when you returned. This environment required vigilance and responsibility, lessons I carried far beyond the school years.

Despite the challenges, I made lifelong friends, including Martin Izevbokun, Uwa Imarhiagbe, Isaac Agboson, Richard

Legema, Edward Traore, Susan Richards, Efe Akpokinovo, McDonald Igbinedion, and Osaze Inneh, among others. Some of the bonds I formed during those years remain strong to this day. Living in that shared space and balancing my responsibilities helped me grow as an individual. Polytechnic life forced me to mature quickly. I also came to understand that my actions had consequences. Everything I did eventually got to my father, whether through official reports or word of mouth. This awareness of this "report card" kept me grounded, even when freedom tempted me to stray.

In my first year, I struggled a bit, finding it hard to maintain the discipline instilled in me back home. But by the second year, I found my rhythm. I refocused, regained my stride, and excelled in my studies. I graduated with an Ordinary National Diploma (OND) in Quantity Surveying, earning an upper credit. This was a proud moment for my family and me, a testament to my perseverance and the support system I had built around me. That sense of freedom I had tasted at Polytechnic stayed with me, but I knew it would not last forever. By this time, my parents were getting older.

My dad had retired and turned his attention to farming. I foresaw that if I went back home during the vacation, inevitably, I would end up doing some agricultural work. As much as I admired my dad's work ethic and dedication, I was not excited about spending the vacation tilling the soil. This realization encouraged me to maximize my time and resources while attending school.

Polytechnic wasn't just about academics; it was a crucible for growth, resilience, and discovery. My years at the Poly shaped me and taught me lessons I continue to cherish and apply today. One of the most admirable aspects of my education was the opportunity to apply the theoretical knowledge I gained in the classroom.

I gained first-hand experience in Quantity Surveying through a four-month internship in Anambra State, which successfully combined theoretical tuition with practical work, deepening my knowledge and appreciation of the profession. When I returned to school, I realized I had an edge over my peers in understanding the concepts taught in class. This initial edge boosted my confidence and reenergized my passion for Quantity Surveying.

A BOLD STEP MOVING TO LAGOS

After completing my OND, I returned home to Benin City, where I noticed a construction site near my street. It was an ELF gas station that was being constructed. One white man was among the people working there, and his presence piqued my curiosity. Mustering my courage, I approached him and inquired about job opportunities.

"I'm just coming from school," I said. "I have an OND. Are

you guys hiring?"

The white man looked at me and asked, "What did you study?"

"I'm a quantity surveyor," I replied.

"Oh, you're a QS?" he said, seeming intrigued. "My brother might need someone like you, but you'll have to go to Lagos to meet him. He owns the company."

These men were from Cyprus, and I could hardly believe my luck. The man handed me his business card. On the back, he wrote his brother's name and their company's address. "Panayotu Panayotis," I read. He continued, "Go to this address and meet my brother, Vanna Vannavas." I was excited, so I sped home and told my dad. My enthusiasm was met with his characteristic realism.

"You wish to travel to Lagos with an OND?" he questioned. "Don't you know that there are people with master's degrees in Lagos who are yet to be employed? All you need is to study a bit more, my friend. Go and take a seat. Finish your HND or pursue a bachelor's degree before you can arrange for Lagos."

I was disappointed but not discouraged. This was something I could not abandon. I informed my mum about it, and she was more inclined to listen to me. Three weeks later, I embarked on a low-profile trip to Lagos.

THE FEAR OF THE UNKNOWN

That journey to Lagos was one of the most terrifying things

I have ever done. I'd never been to Lagos before and knew nothing about the city, but I had an address and a business card. That was enough for me to leap. I traveled on a night bus, my heart racing with a mix of excitement and fear. When I arrived in Lagos, I knew it was not the same as Benin City. The crowded city engulfed me, and I was lost. With only the address to guide me, I wandered through the streets, seeking directions and hoping that everything would go well.

Finally, I reached the location, exhausted and without an idea what lay ahead. It was evening, and I had nowhere to go. Upon examining the business card, it struck the security man that I was telling him the truth. But he was not yet prepared to believe me completely. Instead of bringing me to the building, he dropped me off on the floor at the entrance gate.

The following day, Mr. Vanavas visited me, spotted me, and questioned me about why I had been there. "He paid you a visit, sir," somebody told me, waking me up. I woke up to find a group of people in front of me. Arriving in Lagos with no set plan was daunting and enlightening. I quickly learned how to tackle the complexities of the city with my determination and resourcefulness.

The opportunity I was searching for enabled me to work for VITA Construction Limited, save, and eventually sponsor myself to attend a Higher National Diploma school. My experience in Lagos was eye-opening. It is a large, fast-paced city with a high population density. I lived in Oregun, Ikeja, and made new friends in the neighborhood as well as at the company. I was very young and ambitious, so my ultimate goal was to succeed. It was three years of self-learning, along with mistakes and challenges. My cousin, Mrs. Imwonghomwen Imafidon, lived in the Ogba neighborhood with her family at the time. Spending some weekends at my cousin's apartment helped keep me sane and reduced my feelings of homesickness. At the end of most visits, she would prepare some sauce for me to take to Oregun, such as Egusi soup, Ogbolor soup, and beef stew.

Working at VITA Construction prepared me for my Higher National Diploma (HND) education. I learned the practical aspect of quantity surveying. The experience was priceless and resourceful because of the diversity of the several projects I worked on and supervised. The financial freedom was a plus. I did not make much, but I also did not lack for anything. Suddenly, I began to experience the advantages and privileges that come with success. I made it a challenge to continue striving for success and be more disciplined in all aspects of life.

After spending three years in Lagos, I returned to Auchi Polytechnic to complete my Higher National Diploma (HND). By this time, I had matured significantly, and my experiences in Lagos renewed my focus. During this period, I met my wife, Emily, a freshman at the Polytechnic, and I, a junior. I introduced myself, "Hey, my name is Eric." "My name is Emily." She responded. Curious, I asked, "What is your native name?" She said, "My name is Efosa." I smiled and said, "Oh, my name is Erumwunse." She laughed as I pointed out the coincidence, saying, "That's interesting. Both our names start with E." Without hesitation, I added, "I'm going to marry you." She looked at me incredulously. "Are you crazy? You just met me four days ago! And you're talking about marriage?"

I replied calmly, "Jokes apart, I know what I want. If you're not ready yet, that's fine, but I'm just letting you know." She dismissed me with, "Get out; you don't know what you're saying. You've only just met me." But deep down, I meant every word. I even joked, "Oh, by the way, when we have kids, all of them will have names starting with E.." She shook her head and said, "What is wrong with you?" "I know what I'm saying," I told her confidently.

From the moment we met, I was sure she was the one. While she initially dismissed my confident declarations about our future, our bond grew stronger over time. Emily and I became close friends during our school years, and I eventually won her over. Guess what? That's precisely what happened. All our children ended up with names beginning with E.

During this period, I was finding my footing and beginning to thrive. I had gained independence, sponsored myself, and lived a life I never imagined. After spending three years in Lagos, I returned to Benin a changed man. To my family and peers, I was like someone from a foreign land. I had money, confidence, and a sense of accomplishment. Even my clothes were a testament to my new status. If you wore Lagos clothing, people could instantly tell it wasn't made locally in Benin.

My siblings benefited from my success, too, as I shared some of my proceeds and blessings with them. However, during my time at HND, a cultural phenomenon was sweeping through this idea of "Andrew, I want to check out." This was a euphemism for people leaving the country to seek greener pastures abroad. Everyone wanted to "check out." I saw friends from my neighborhood reappearing after a few months in Germany, Austria, or the UK, sending home cars and money. I was inspired and decided to follow that path.

Unfortunately, this was my first significant mistake and roadblock. I told Emily, my then-girlfriend, about my plan, and she was disappointed. "Why don't you just finish school first?" she pleaded. But I was determined. I told her, "I'll finish school over there. I'll make money, and I'll send it to you. We'll marry, don't worry." It all sounded so easy in my head. With Germany as my final destination, I secured a visa to Hungary and paid someone to handle the process.

Everything seemed ready except for one thing: I was

short 3,200 Naira for the ticket. That amount was significant at the time and was all the money I had saved. I approached my father for help. "Dad, I need 3,200 Naira for my ticket. I've done everything else." My father was unimpressed. "Before getting a passport, didn't you know you'd need money for a ticket? Why didn't you plan for this?" I explained, "I thought I could handle it, but I ended up paying someone to process everything, and now I'm short."

He shook his head. "I don't have that kind of money," he said firmly. "Do you know how many people with master's degrees in Lagos don't have jobs? Do you think you'll succeed abroad with an OND? Just focus on finishing your studies first." I was devastated. I turned to my mother, hoping to persuade him, but she couldn't change his mind. In fairness, my father didn't have the money, nor was he the type to take risks by borrowing.

Frustrated and angry, I left home. I moved in with a friend on Uwasota Street, Benin City, and decided not to return to school. I was convinced I would find another way to leave for Germany. Unfortunately, my plans fell apart, and I lost an entire school year. Eventually, I came to my senses and returned to complete my HND.

It was not easy because I returned to school to be classmates with students who were far junior to me. Emily, who had been with me since day one, was proud of me for returning. Considering how adamant I had been about quitting the country, she had assumed that I'd never be going back to school.

Despite the detour and the year lost, I finished my HND. Having that done was a victory for me. It started my career and mended my relationship with my father. That moment was a learning experience in patience, planning, and persistence. It reminded me that failures are not the end of the road. They are just part of the process. Today, I am grateful for what has occurred because it has shaped me into who I am.

After completing my HND, I was sent to Taraba State for my National Youth Service Corps (NYSC) program. My dream to move abroad moved me to change my deployment to Lagos, where I believed I would have access to more opportunities. This marked the beginning of a new chapter in my life. My dream of working or studying abroad was finally realized. I moved to Europe, where I worked and lived in Spain and Ukraine. There, I studied languages and practiced multiculturalism.

I won the United States Diversity Visa Lottery and immigrated to Des Moines, Iowa, in 2000. When I arrived in the United States, I faced new challenges, including having my HND evaluated as equivalent to a high school diploma. Initially disheartened, I returned to school and earned an MBA from the University of Phoenix. I later pursued advanced studies in Industrial and Organizational Psychology, earning a Master's degree and eventually a PhD.

THE LEGACY OF EDUCATION

Education has always been a cornerstone of my family's identity. My siblings and I have all pursued higher education, and my children carry on this tradition. They understand that education is not just a stepping stone towards other successes, but a legacy in and of itself, defined by drive and tenacity.

Throughout my life, mentors and role models have played a significant role in my development. From my father, who instilled the value of learning, to professors and peers, each of them has helped shape my path. Today, as both a parent and a professional, I strive to be a living role model, demonstrating to my children and the broader public that any accomplishment is possible through hard work and a desire to learn.

My most influential role model was my father. He always stressed that education is the pathway to success and is the most certain way out of poverty. He possessed a profound understanding of this fact, and he was correct. His insight and wisdom had a profound impact on my resolve to pursue academic and personal excellence.

Another mentor who profoundly impacted me during college was Mr. Joseph Campbell, who has now passed away. He was a lecturer at Auchi Polytechnic and a standout educator. He had been trained in the UK, specifically at Glasgow, through a "train the trainer" program. When he returned, he brought that same rigor and philosophy into the classroom, which shaped my learning experience during my HND.

Mr. Campbell taught me the idea of "studying smart, not hard," an expression he had learned while in the United Kingdom. He was brilliant at avoiding unnecessary complications. His teaching method was simple yet effective, always emphasizing the value of simplicity and practicality. This philosophy was also evident in his personal life: on most mornings, he wore slippers or flip-flops to school, which confused some of us students.

When asked why he wore such footwear, he would just shrug and say, "I'm comfortable in this." This way of life taught us the value of simplicity in both our academic pursuits and our personal lives. My brother is another significant influence in my life, despite being 10 years younger than I am. Given his youth, he has demonstrated incredible resilience and grit, qualities that continue to inspire me to this day.

His life is one filled with stories that could fill ten books. He has overcome numerous challenges to build a highly successful life in the United Kingdom. At one point, he stayed with me in Ukraine before moving to Italy and eventually settling in the UK. Today, he is thriving. I'll never forget how he supported me during my time in Europe. He even sent me money to buy my first cell phone while I was in Spain, when he was in Italy. We've always maintained a close relationship, and I can count on him for ideas, support, and wisdom.

He knows me so well that he can finish my sentences, and if anyone wanted to know more about me, he'd be the one to call. Though younger than me, he is a role model in his own right. From him, I've learned the power of resilience and determination. In my professional life, I've also had the privilege of being mentored by remarkable individuals. One such person is Mark Omen, whom I met at Wells Fargo church.

Mark mentored me for three years while serving as the head of the Wells Fargo Market. What stood out most about him was his simplicity and pragmatism. He taught me how to aim for excellence while staying grounded. One of his most impactful lessons was that "empty vessels make the loudest noise." This statement has stayed with me, reminding me to focus on substance rather than appearance.

I must acknowledge Pastor Richard Webb, a valued mentor whose guidance was instrumental throughout my Ph.D. studies. We met regularly to discuss my progress and challenges, and his unwavering encouragement helped me stay focused and determined. Pastor Richard taught me to integrate faith and purpose into my research and studies, enriching my academic journey. His wealth of knowledge, diverse perspectives, and unwavering support enriched my journey in countless ways.

My mentors—my dad, Mr. Campbell, my younger brother, Mr. Omen, and Pastor Webb—each contributed uniquely to my development. Their lessons have shaped my outlook on education, resilience, and the importance of simplicity in achieving greatness.

Education has remained a central theme throughout my life. After completing my MBA, I returned to school to pursue a degree in psychology. I was deeply interested in understanding human behavior, why people act the way they do, and why some are kind while others seem cruel or indifferent. I was also curious about the workplace dynamics, the diversity of personalities, and how those dynamics influence outcomes.

Psychology fascinated me because it addressed these questions. I also delved into ethical intelligence, a subject I was naturally drawn to because I believed in the importance of procedural fairness. I've always advocated for treating people kindly but fairly, ensuring transparent and equitable processes. This passion for fairness became a cornerstone of my education and personal philosophy.

Balancing education as an adult was no easy feat. I was a parent, a working professional, and a soccer dad all at the same time. However, I pushed through because I wanted to set a good example for my children. I wanted them to know that they had no excuse for not striving to be their best. Pursuing a Master's or Ph.D. isn't a requirement, but choosing not to pursue excellence shouldn't stem from the belief that it's impossible.

I earned my Master of Public Administration (M.P.A.)

and a Master of Public Health from Walden University in Minnesota. I told myself, "Why stop here? Let me go all the way." Therefore, I decided to pursue a Ph.D. in Industrial-Organizational Psychology. The journey was not without challenges. It was long and filled with obstacles, such as parenting duties, running an orphanage, and helping my children through school. But I never gave up, and when I finally received my doctorate, it was surreal to hear people call me "Dr. Eric." Occasionally, I even caught myself forgetting that they were talking about me.

Earning my Ph.D. was a source of great pride. I regretted that my father was not alive to see me accomplish this objective. I knew that he would have felt a sense of pride. In many ways, I felt his presence and encouragement throughout my studies. Education is a long-standing family tradition. One of my brothers, who lives in the United Kingdom, recently had the chance to finish his doctorate. The youngest is an engineer with numerous certifications. Each of my siblings has pursued higher education, making my father's dream of an educated family a reality.

Now, my children understand the worth of education because they can see examples of it. They talk about it openly with their peers and among themselves. This legacy of education has become an integral part of our family's DNA, and I couldn't be more proud of it. Throughout school, I became aware of a distinct characteristic within myself: leadership ability. People would typically look to me and request that I lead, organize, or serve as their spokesperson. The feature was so conspicuous that friends called me "EPA," which is short for "old man," in recognition of my adult personality despite my boyish years. While at the Polytechnic, I developed my leadership skills as president of the Ophelia Club, a civic club similar to the Rotary or Lions Club. During my time in office, the club was highly engaged in acts of charity, including periodic trips to orphanages.

I remember a trip to Nigeria, during which we toured the Orphanage in Edo and met a boy we named David Ophelia. We decided to sponsor him and send him money and essentials for many years. That encounter planted a seed in my heart; it evoked a sense of responsibility toward orphans and a duty to care for them. I remember asking, "Why would someone go through the joy and pain of birth only to give the child up?" This was at the back of my mind, shaping my perception of parenthood and charity.

I cannot condemn anyone for giving their child up for adoption because I do not understand their background. Hence, I employed empathy and love to calm my soul without focusing on why a child had been abandoned. As president of the Ophelia Club, I emphasized that our efforts cannot be a single occurrence. I told my members, "This has to be a commitment of a few years, even after graduation." I made it my responsibility to ensure that future club leadership would carry on the tradition of giving back.

This experience left a lasting impression on me. Years later, when my wife and I were struggling to have children, we prayed and promised God: "If You give us one child, we will adopt one. If You give us two, we'll adopt two." God answered our prayer, blessing us with three boys in quick succession. Adopting three children at that time seemed too overwhelming, so we channeled our vow into sponsoring orphanages instead.

During a trip to Nigeria in 2003, I visited two orphanages. Neither met my expectations, so I decided to start my own. I had never studied how to run a nonprofit, but my experience with the Ophelia Club provided the necessary foundation for me to do so.

In 2004, I transformed part of my parents' property from a modest "face me, I face you" house into a self-contained orphanage facility. My original plan was to build a retirement home for my parents, but after my father passed away and my mother could not live there alone, I repurposed the space for an orphanage.

Thus, the Orphanage was born. It has been one of the most rewarding endeavors of my life. The experience with Baby David in Edo Orphanage planted the seed, but my faith and life watered it. I believe the best way to worship God is to love one another. It is not in the grand things; it is in meeting people's needs, feeding the hungry, clothing the naked, giving shelter to the homeless, and caring for the vulnerable. Every time we do these things, we answer God's prayer, "To love one another." This philosophy has guided my life, and I hope it will inspire others to follow my example.

THE BUILDING BLOCK OF MY CAREER

My first official job came during my internship at Auchi Polytechnic. After completing the first year, all students were sent to companies in their respective fields of study to gain hands-on experience. I was assigned to Nwanbueze Ogbuefi and Associates, a consulting Quantity Surveying firm. This was a significant moment for me as it required me to travel from my home state, Edo State, to Enugu in eastern Nigeria. At that time, I was about 19 years old. Upon arriving in Enugu, the company informed me that they didn't have accommodations in the city. Instead, they decided the best way to learn would be to send me to one of their active project sites. The site in question was the construction of the Federal Polytechnic Ado-Ekiti, a project under their supervision. This meant traveling west, from the East to the Midwest and beyond.

This was a daunting journey. In Enugu, the dominant language was Igbo, while in Ado-Ekiti, it was Yoruba, neither of which I spoke nor understood. When I arrived in Ado-Ekiti, the resident quantity surveyor, Chris, who had been informed of my posting, welcomed me. Chris took me in and provided a thorough orientation and induction into practical quantity surveying.

The internship was designed to teach me the economics of construction, including reading blueprints and applying theory from the classroom to real-world situations. The on-the-job training was invaluable. It grounded me in the realities of the marketplace and gave me an insider's appreciation of how the theory we learned in class was translated into actual building projects. I connected the gap between theory and practice during the four-month program and the subsequent holiday period.

I was more confident and prepared when I returned to school after my internship. I could relate classroom lessons to what I had seen and done on-site, which made me much more engaged in my studies. After completing my OND, my first post-graduation job was with Vita Construction Ltd. in Lagos. This opportunity came about serendipitously. While at home in Benin, I noticed the company was constructing a gas station at the corner of the street leading to my house.

I walked up to the site and spoke to the site engineer, a white man from Cyprus. After explaining my qualifications, he told me that his brother, who was in charge, was based in Lagos. He handed me a business card and encouraged me to visit their office in Lagos. I did not hesitate to take advantage of the opportunity to go to Lagos. Since childhood, I have never feared learning or doing things incorrectly. I believe that one learns by doing. Upon my arrival at the Lagos office, I greeted Mr. Barnabas, who owns the company, and he was impressed with my willingness and work ethic.

I joined the company with the practical skills I had gained from my internship, which immediately set me apart from others. At the time, the company had a Quantity Surveyor (a graduate with a Higher National Diploma - HND) working for them, but he was let go due to concerns about his work ethic. I stepped in, even though I had only an Ordinary National Diploma (OND), equivalent to an associate degree in the U.S. Despite my humble qualifications, I was given significant responsibilities, including supervising projects worth millions of Naira.

My work involved more than just calculations from drawings. I had to ensure that the expected costs matched the on-site prices. I also broke down exceptions or deviations and justified them. It was a difficult job, but it was also fulfilling. As a young professional, I was earning well and enjoying a newfound independence. Unlike when I was in Benin under my father's watchful eye, I now had the freedom to explore and grow.

From 1986 to 1989, I worked on several high-profile

projects at Vita Construction. One of my key assignments was supervising the construction of Double Three Beer's factory in Akure. The second was Eko Holiday Inn Cottage 18, an upscale development. I also worked on two major projects in Victoria Island, a new development sector where reclaimed land was being developed into high-quality properties.

These projects posed challenges that tested my professional boundaries, enabling me to expand my capabilities in project management and large-scale building projects. They were not easy projects, but learning experiences. Reflecting on these early work experiences, they laid the groundwork for my career. They taught me the value of persistence, flexibility, and courage in exploring possibilities, even in uncharted territory.

During my one-year service with the National Youth Service Corps (NYSC) in Lagos, I gained valuable work experience. My first assignment was at GIDA Nigeria Limited on Allen Avenue, Lagos. Before working with GIDA, I worked with NITEL, a telephone organization on Victoria Island. I worked as a quantity surveyor for GIDA Nigeria Limited, and our office handled multiple projects within Lagos. I was more self-assured by this time than ever before and was making progressive strides in my field of endeavor.

Even though I sometimes made mistakes, I never lost the opportunity to learn and continued to excel at each new challenge. I felt an exceptional sense of accomplishment growing, as I could confidently advance into new responsibilities with ease. Suddenly, I decided to take the big leap: to go abroad and pursue overseas opportunities.

My sojourn was in Kyiv, Ukraine. My first job was a lesson in humility: I had to begin anew. The language was the biggest challenge for me. It was neither Edo nor Yoruba; it was Russian. I initially learned Russian on the streets, which was a mistake. I accidentally picked up the slang and obscene expressions, and was embarrassed when I started working in proper settings.

Before finding a job, I worked on a farm for a few months. Physical labor was tiring, especially during Ukraine's winter months. Experiencing temperatures as low as 78°F in Nigeria and dealing with temperatures that fell to as low as -15°C proved to be a shock. I quickly learned that farm life was not feasible, so I scouted for something that accommodated my qualifications.

Subsequently, I secured a position with New Century Holdings, an American company based in Kyiv, specializing in real estate and construction. My background in quantity surveying proved beneficial, and I was hired to assist with procuring commercial properties. I did my work well, but struggled to communicate effectively. The Russian I had learned on the streets included slang and inappropriate phrases, making office life difficult. Observing this, I resolved to learn Russian, focusing on mastering the language through reading, writing, and speaking.

I quickly realized that I was different. Being a black man in a predominantly white culture in the early 1990s wasn't fun. Diversity was lacking, and respect for individuals of color was absent. I experienced racism and harsh treatment, sometimes humiliating. What kept me going was my faith, my childhood experience, how I was raised, tenacity, and the desire to succeed.

Life in Ukraine was filled with struggles. I left Nigeria for Europe in search of greener pastures, but upon arriving in Kyiv, I quickly realized that life would not be easy. The food, language, weather, people, culture, technology, social life, and the absence of family felt unfamiliar. Back home in Nigeria, I was accustomed to staple foods like rice, cassava, and yam. In Kyiv, besides rice, most African foods were unavailable to me. We had to improvise, replacing Egusi soup with beef stew thickened with egg and using flour as a substitute for cassava and yam.

It was two years of my stay in Kyiv before I tasted Egusi soup again. My friend Moses had gone to Nigeria, and when he returned, he brought a whole load of food. That day was like Christmas or the World Cup, and it was then that I realized how much I had missed the flavors of home. Moses shared some of his food with me willingly, and since then, we have been close friends, a bond that remains strong to this day.

By the late 1990s, as more people of African descent migrated to Kyiv, African foods became more accessible, making life a little easier for those of us longing for a taste of home.

There were times when I had to provide shelter for some stranded Nigerians. However, I had some unpleasant experiences with a few of the people whom I had sheltered. The kind gesture allowed me to understand certain human behaviors. When you do good, do not expect a good treat in response! I acquired some debts because I wanted to help people.

During my stay in Ukraine, I became close to some friends I call family. They include Margaret Amadin, McDonald Igbinedion, Victor Imokhuede, Ede, Austin Stone, Nosa, Bayo Olaiya, Solomon Agbonavbare, etc. Emily joined me in Kyiv in 1997. At first, she was thrilled with her experience with the snow and cold. But she struggled with the language and discrimination.

We got married at the Church of the Nazarene in Kyiv on September 28, 2007. It was a double celebration because Emily's birthday was September 28. We have a 2-in-1 celebration every year: our wedding anniversary and Emily's birthday. Emily and I were no longer enjoying ourselves in Kyiv, so we relocated to another country. We settled on Spain.

Throughout my five years in Kyiv, I worked for New Century Holdings for roughly three years before shifting to

Spain in 1997. Moving to Madrid was a new challenge. I once again found myself with a language handicap, as Spanish was unknown. Additionally, the procedures and systems in Spain differed, and I had to complete significant paperwork to adapt to the new infrastructure.

My first job in Spain was working in a garden. Thank you to the Malon family for providing me with a work contract. The work reminded me of my childhood, but I was resilient this time. It wasn't easy; it took many hours and was hard work, but I persevered. I was encouraged by recollections of working around a small backyard garden as a kid in Nigeria, though on a much larger scale.

A few months later, I started working in restaurants. I labored briefly at Planet Hollywood in Madrid before transitioning to construction work. These labor-based jobs required hard work, but they sustained me financially. Throughout the following two years, I learned to appreciate resilience, perseverance, and a stubborn will to succeed.

As the firstborn in my family, I felt a significant responsibility to succeed. Numerous members of my household relied upon me, particularly my younger siblings, who were in college. I also provided them with small amounts of money. Such continuous reliance on me was one of the factors that pushed me to work even harder.

My life in Madrid was both exciting and frustrating. The

frustration stemmed from adapting to life's struggles, work, language differences, and the stress that accompanies the obligation of gratitude I owe to my family. However, the spirit of football—soccer brought me joy almost every weekend. It was like therapy. Although I lived in Madrid, I supported Football Club Barcelona, the team with the biggest rivalry with Real Madrid. I am still a big fan of F.C. Barcelona!

As a black man, I was treated relatively better in Madrid compared to my experience in Kyiv. The discrimination was evident, and being different was an issue. I experienced discrimination both at work and within the community. I was able to handle this challenge because of my experience in Kyiv.

I am not very fluent in Spanish, as it is not my native language, so my wife and I attended an interdenominational service in Madrid. That is where we met the family of Mr. and Mrs. Ivan Concepcion and their two children, Natalia and Fernando. They are Americans; Ivan worked for Principal Financial Group. We became family friends and supported each other. Crossing paths with the Concepcions was not a coincidence. It was a divine intervention. You will see why this is true as you read the entire book.

My family and I relocated to the United States in 2000. As our starting point, we chose Des Moines, Iowa, influenced by our family friends, Mr. and Mrs. Ivan Concepcion, whom we met in Madrid. Moving to the U.S. was a dream come true, something I had longed for since watching Soul Train and MTV as a child in Nigeria. I imagined a life filled with opportunities, success, and the vibrant culture I saw on TV. We were told that in America, you are not allowed to spank your kids. Emily and I grew up with spanking as a means of correction. We are aware of some of the challenges in big cities, such as New York, Atlanta, Chicago, Los Angeles, Detroit, and Miami, so we decided to search for a smaller, quieter city.

I asked our friend Mr. Concepcion for help. He recommended Des Moines, Iowa. He offered to introduce us to his church family, the Lutheran Church of Hope, in Des Moines. We accepted the offer, and he introduced us to Pastor Mike Hosholder and Pastor John Kline. After a few correspondences, we quickly realized that Mr. Conception & family were put on our path or life journey wasn't a coincidence but God's purpose. The church purchased the air tickets for my family.

When my family arrived at the Des Moines airport on September 7, 2000, members of the Lutheran Church of Hope welcomed us. It was a very warm welcome on a freezing day. Approximately 15 to 20 church members, led by Pastor John Kline, were present. They held balloons and signs that said, "The Idehen family, welcome to the United States." The church also provided other items, including a two-bedroom apartment in West Des Moines, a Toyota Camry, clothing, furniture, beds and bedding, food items, a refrigerator, a television, and toys for children. The first day of our new home/apartment experience was overwhelming. I was worried about what the church would charge us for these items because I didn't have the money to pay for them. So, I asked Pastor Kline about the obligation and cost.

He said it was all free. The church would suggest that we pay it forward whenever we are presented with such an opportunity. His response shocked me because I had never experienced such a magnitude of God's grace. Also, the church's kind gesture reaffirmed my faith in God. Lutheran Church of Hope is a church that is after God's heart. We became church members in 2001 and still are to this day. The church is our immediate family in the United States. The men's group members, "Pretty Interesting Guys Stuff- P.I.G.S," are my Brothers in Christ!

Through the church, adjusting to the new environment in Des Moines was smooth and easy compared to the other places we have lived. It opens doors to opportunities because many people are watching over you. However, reality hit hard when we arrived in Des Moines. Despite my degree and professional background, I couldn't find a job in quantity surveying because the profession didn't exist in the same way in the U.S. I had to explain what it was, but it didn't come out as I intended. With no other option, I was a dishwasher at Dahl's Food in

November 2000. This job was far from the glamorous life I had envisioned. Mopping floors, doing dishes, and sometimes helping with serving lunches were modest tasks.

Occasionally, I was disappointed and told my wife we might have to return to Europe. A spontaneous chance did come up at this job, though. While working in the kitchen, I used to converse with customers in Spanish, Russian, and my Nigerian languages, Edo and pidgin English. One customer who worked for Wells Fargo would often notice my language skills and engage in conversation.

She would ask me repeatedly how I was doing, and one day, I simply told her, "Not good." Curious, she asked me why. I explained to her that I did not enjoy the work and was open to being reassigned. She asked me if I would be open to working in a bank, to which I quickly replied, "Yes! Do you train?" She informed me that Wells Fargo would train me and that I should submit my application. The lady's name was Ms. Diane Brown, now Mrs. Diane Porter.

Back then, applications were paper-based rather than online, so I completed and submitted the paperwork. That interaction marked the beginning of a new chapter in my journey, as I transitioned from washing dishes to building a professional career in the United States.

I did it. She interviewed me, and I remember she offered me coffee. She asked, "Do you want coffee?" I said yes because

I thought declining would hurt my chances. She gave me the coffee, and as I drank it, I was shaking, sweating, and visibly uncomfortable. But she didn't notice and started the interview. Her only question was, "Tell me about your life in Europe."

I asked her how much time I had, and she replied, "10 minutes." I then provided her with a brief overview of my life in Ukraine, Spain, and the United States. That was the entire interview; no questions were asked about my strengths or weaknesses, or detailed scenarios, such as "Tell me about a time you faced a challenge and how you handled it." She simply asked about my life in Europe and wrapped up the interview.

When I got home, I told my wife, "The interview lasted only 10 minutes. She didn't ask me any of the usual questions. I think I messed it up." My wife reassured me, "You might be surprised. She could still call you." Emily was right. I got the call a few days later, and she offered me the job. In 2001, I officially joined Wells Fargo as a front-line teller. I met the hiring manager, Diane Brown (later Diane Porter), during orientation. Curious, I asked her why she had hired me. She smiled and said, "I wanted to give you the opportunity because I believe you deserve more."

From that day forward, I called her my "sister from another mother." She was white, and I was black, so people often questioned our connection, but to me, she was family and still is today.

I spent a year and a half as a teller, handling various bank transactions for our customers and learning the basics of banking. Due to my language skills, I transitioned into a customer service representative role at one of our offices. I have moved between several offices, gaining experience and honing my skills. Later, I was promoted to a banking position, where I dealt with customers, profiled them, and introduced them to various banking products and services, including account opening and credit card issuance.

As a green card holder, I would be eligible for U.S. citizenship in five years. I also wanted to be a part of African American culture, so I joined the team member network group called CheckPoint, which later became Black African American Connections (BAAC). I aimed to learn about Juneteenth, Black History Month, and other aspects of African American culture. While I identified as Nigerian American, I was often called African American, and I wanted to embrace and understand this part of my identity.

I also volunteered for Wells Fargo events celebrating various cultures, including Latino and Asian events. I joined the Latino network group HOLA (Organization for Latino Advancement) to keep practicing my Spanish. Additionally, I joined the Asian Connection of Iowa not because I spoke any Asian languages but because I believed understanding someone's culture was essential for effective management and building relationships, whether as a manager or colleague.

Wells Fargo noticed my commitment and interest. Sometime later, an opening for a community development officer became available. The job involved building relationships within the community, learning about banking products and services, and feeling confident in representing the bank to the community.

One day, I was called by a friend who insisted, "Eric, you should apply for this job." My first instinct was, "I don't think I'm there yet." But after looking at their salary, I replied, "Why not?" So, I applied. To my surprise, I got the job. My volunteerism and consistent performance in retail banking significantly contributed to this promotion. I transitioned from a teller to a community development officer. We consistently exceeded expectations.

Wells Fargo's performance reviews ranked employees on a five-point scale, where level four represented "consistently above expectations." I consistently achieved level four. This was made possible through what my dad taught me. He would constantly remind me, "Don't settle for less. Always arm yourself with more." Growing up in a tough neighborhood where being resourceful and resilient was essential for survival, I developed a temperament that drove me to strive for excellence. For example, if the company's target were 20 monthly sales, I would aim for 40. Even if I didn't reach 40, I exceeded the company's target, typically selling between 28 and 30. This strategy worked for me in retail banking, where new goals and challenges arose daily. I applied this strategy in my role as a community development officer, where I established a strong rapport with the community and helped individuals connect with the bank's services and resources.

While I worked at Wells Fargo, we received a series of awards. One thing that stands out is that we were awarded Corporate Diversity Organization of the Year. A standout project I contributed to in Des Moines was the HOLA Center. The project aimed to foster a closer relationship between Wells Fargo and the Latino community. It was a collaboration with various service providers, businesses, and agencies, including the police department, visiting nurses, and some of the critical services that the Latino community uses daily. We made it a one-stop shop, which we called the HOLA Center.

This project provided me with a new perspective on delivering services tailored to the choices and actual needs of low- and moderate-income communities. Over the course of four years, we developed the HOLA Center as part of Wells Fargo's Community Reinvestment Act (CRA) efforts. Under the CRA, regulators require banks to reinvest in the communities where they operate and meet specific performance standards. In Iowa, Wells Fargo has consistently earned the highest scores from regulators, such as the FDIC, in Community Reinvestment

Act (CRA) tests. When Wells Fargo floundered nationwide, Iowa ranked higher in performance. While I don't claim full credit, the efforts I led played a significant role in the outcome.

TRANSITION TO DIVERSITY LEADERSHIP

In 2009, an excellent opportunity arose at Wells Fargo Financial, a division of Wells Fargo Bank N.A., to serve as a Diversity Director. The department primarily serviced retailer credit relationships with companies such as Menards and Best Buy, and operated other partner businesses. The role required a person with banking experience, community engagement experience, and the capability to work across cultural differences to promote organizational diversity.

I transitioned into my first leadership role in diversity specialization, becoming the vice president, which was an exciting and life-altering experience. As Diversity Director, my responsibilities included increasing workplace motivation, adherence to employment opportunity legislation, and streamlining hiring, retention, and promotion practices. At that time, the focus was on diversity and inclusion (DEI); equity had not yet been formally added to the model.

I gained new strategies and valuable knowledge about diplomacy, particularly when working with senior leaders, such as C-suite executives. I wanted to institute change immediately, but I was too confrontational in my approach, insisting on immediate results. I quickly found that it wasn't working. I adjusted my strategy, taking the time to sit down one-on-one with leaders from all lines of business. I listened to their personal diversity experiences, built relationships, and gained their buy-in. This collaboration took off, and I worked with the president of Wells Fargo Financial and other senior executive leaders to successfully roll out DEI initiatives.

NAVIGATING ORGANIZATIONAL CHANGES

There were significant changes after three years in my role at Wells Fargo. Wells Fargo acquired Wachovia, which brought new leadership and a more expansive diversity, equity, and inclusion (DEI) framework, resulting in job redundancies. My role as Diversity Director became redundant.

Additionally, Wells Fargo Financial, a division with a 111-year legacy, was dissolved as part of the company's restructuring. Our 19,000 employees were either absorbed or let go to accommodate Wachovia's significantly larger employee pool, which employs over 100,000 employees.

As Diversity Director, I managed DEI efforts in the U.S., Canada, Puerto Rico, and Guam. However, Wachovia's international presence extended beyond that, with Europe playing a key role in the reorganization.

A NEW CHAPTER IN MY CAREER

After leaving Wells Fargo, I joined Bank of the West (now BMO) as a Branch Sales Manager. I spent two years there, refining my skills and excelling in leadership roles. Then, I explored the non-profit sector and joined the Boys and Girls Club as a Unit Director.

At the Boys and Girls Club, I managed operations at the George Washington Carver Elementary School in Des Moines. This role allowed me to give back to the community hands-on and provided a fresh perspective on leadership within the non-profit sector. I genuinely enjoy working with children from diverse communities and backgrounds.

After nine months as the Boys and Girls Club's unit director, Wells Fargo contacted me. They needed someone who could hit the ground running to return as a Community Development Officer, a role I had previously held before transitioning to the position of Diversity Director. In 2014, I returned to Wells Fargo as Vice President of Community Development. It felt effortless to return to a familiar position. I leveraged the errors, learnings, and development from my previous experiences to perform more effectively in this role. We were doing well, and everything was going as it should. However, when I was expecting to be promoted to Senior Vice President, I encountered a snag. Even though I worked hard and pleaded, the promotion did not happen. I put the situation into perspective and found that it might not be enough even with an MBA.

I pursued more education and a master's degree in Industrial and Organizational Psychology. I was interested in learning more about human behavior, particularly in workplace settings. After gaining experience working with diverse populations and individuals in various settings, I sought to study the science of human behavior and interaction between individuals and organizations. Work is complex, and the equation can lead to issues when combined with human complexity.

I considered Industrial and Organizational Psychology to be the field that could fill that space. It also overlaps with Human Resources (HR), which traditionally carried a negative stigma. Based on what some people believed was HR's overemphasis on representing employers over employees, organizations changed their name to Employee Relations. However, even with this rebranding, the mistrust persisted. I-O Psychology provides a framework for holding HR or Employee Relations accountable, ensuring they fulfill their intended roles.

After completing my master's, I decided to take the next step and pursue a PhD in the same field. In doing so, Wells Fargo fired me just before the COVID-19 pandemic. A new management plan was to reduce the workforce by 30,000 employees over three years, with 10,000 jobs being cut annually. Many doubted it was feasible, but the cuts were swift, and I was among the first wave to be let go.

A NEW CHAPTER OF EMBRACING COMMUNITY RELATIONS

During the pandemic, I joined AmeriFirst Mortgage, which is headquartered in Kalamazoo, Michigan. Though significantly smaller than Wells Fargo, this role was among the best I've ever had. I was hired as the Community Relations Director, overseeing initiatives nationwide. Amerifirst Mortgage was owned by two individuals and focused solely on mortgages.

Despite being a smaller organization, the compensation exceeded what I had earned at Wells Fargo, and I thoroughly enjoyed the work. My role emphasized reimbursing the community and building authentic customer relationships. Marketing is secondary when you care for your people and treat your customers right. Word-of-mouth from customers is worth more than gold.

My service was not professional; it was personal. I relate to my clients, individuals who are struggling to better themselves. That got me through, and my work was genuinely appreciated. Then, I kept returning to Nigeria, my native land, and remaining at the orphanage we set up. Each time I came, I lamented the state of the economy, the lack of infrastructure, and the meager growth rate. My friends in Nigeria grew tired of listening to me lament. One day, during a conversation, someone told me, "Eric, you come here, you complain, and then you return to the United States to enjoy your life. The next time you come, the problems have worsened, and you complain again. Who is going to fix it?"

That question, "Who's going to do it?" nagged at me momentarily. I tried to wave it off, explaining, "You boys need to fix it." But they replied, "That's where you are wrong. You must return and participate with others with true, good intentions and fix it." That conversation was a wake-up call for me. I couldn't shake those words when I returned to America.

I spoke to my wife about the experience; she knew immediately it would become something big. I waved it off at first, explaining to her that it was only a conversation. But deep in my heart, I knew it was something more significant. I told her two months later, "I need to return to Nigeria and run for office." She asked why, and I explained, "People are coming to the orphanage to beg for food. My staff said, 'Sir, let's not give them rice,' but I insisted, 'Give it to them.' I can't keep doing this over and over. I'm getting tired. I need a platform to access resources to help the larger community."

I decided to pursue a career in politics and resigned from my job on February 8, 2022. The job I resigned from was the best I ever had. I packed my bags, and my family agreed to support me, though they decided to remain in the U.S. My wife said, "We'll visit you when things settle." I told her, "No problem. When everything is in place, you can join me." Our kids were mostly grown then, so it seemed feasible.

I was unsure whether to mention my past political involvement. Still, I did indicate that I wanted to compete for public office while continuing to serve as a consultant and psychologist. Procedural fairness and moral intelligence are substantial aspects of my personality. Soon enough, I learned in politics and Nigeria that idealism does not count. I joined one of the parties, believing it would be easy. My background and qualifications were more than sufficient.

However, I soon discovered that qualifications did not matter; it was a matter of who you knew and what interests you had. I do not object to personal interests, but when they become selfish, they can be dangerous. This was the first bitter lesson in politics. Looking back, I wouldn't even call it a political career; it was more of a political trial. People now ask me, "Eric, are you a politician?" I always respond, "No, I'm interested in policies, but I'm not a politician yet."

Within two years, I uncovered some of the root causes of Nigeria's political issues. The problem isn't the elected official; the kingmakers—the self-proclaimed leaders—operate in the background. Those are the individuals you rarely see on TV, but they have a significant amount of control. They decide who to nominate, who to run, and who will get elected. You'll never make it unless you have the kingmakers with you, no matter how skilled, intelligent, or talented you are.

Spending two years taking money from me, playing with my delegate list, playing with the system so that I did not receive the party ticket at all, not on merit, but so that I wouldn't be able to move ahead. It all showed that the system and leadership are dysfunctional. There's so much to unpack about my time in politics, like peeling the layers of an onion, but that's a story for another day. After those two years, I returned to the U.S. to rebuild.

Upon my return, I had earned my PhD, but I was met with challenges. I applied for several jobs and kept coming in second. I was told I was overqualified four times, but age and other factors were likely at play, though no one admitted it. I wasn't chosen even for roles I could do with my eyes closed. During this time, I consulted and worked with nonprofits, earning just enough to get by.

Then, I received a call about an opportunity at the Evelyn K. Davis Center for Working Families, a non-profit organization here in Des Moines. They work with working families, inner-city residents, and individuals seeking jobs, aiming to enhance their computer skills, start small businesses, or develop financial literacy. They also help people re-enter society after incarceration.

Although the role was listed as a manager position, I was

familiar with the organization from my time at Wells Fargo. I managed funds for non-profits as part of our Community Reinvestment Act (CRA) initiatives. I applied and got the job. This is my current role. While it doesn't pay what I used to earn, it gives me immense fulfillment. I use everything I've learned over the years to serve our clients.

When people walk through the door, I see myself in them. I was once Eric, who didn't know how to use a computer. When I came to the U.S., I was Eric, who had no credit and thought that paying cash for everything was a good idea. I remember being told, "No, you have to owe to have good credit." That was a learning experience, even though I was working at a bank at the time. I was also Eric, who wanted to start a business but didn't know how to do it.

These experiences shaped how I approach my work today. I founded OPX International, which stands for "Ordinary People doing Extraordinary Things through Good Business." The company, OPX International LLC, is my way of instilling the spirit of entrepreneurship in my children. I've made my eldest son, Enrique, a co-owner and vice president because I want him to learn firsthand what it takes to build and manage a business.

My goal is simple: I don't want my kids to work for anyone else. I want them to work for themselves and create opportunities for others, and we're actively working towards that vision. I'm balancing my work at OPX International with my current role. It's not as lucrative as my previous job at AmeriFirst Mortgage, which I left to pursue a career in politics, but it gives me a deep sense of fulfillment.

This job allows me to serve people and share my story. I tell them, "I was once like you. I have started afresh over four times in life, from nothing to achieving accomplishments, only to lose everything so that I could do it all over somewhere else. Everything that has occurred has made me resilient, humble, and not to surrender. With every new beginning, I have found it significant to keep my head up regardless of what comes.

My professional ethos is based upon an unwavering commitment to improving people's lives and serving systems that build and improve their lives. Whether an employee, an entrepreneur, or a founder of a non-profit organization, I want to be an agent of change. I was deeply influenced by my parents, especially by my father. His guiding principle was always, "If you do it, own it. It is better to own up to a mistake than lie and receive twice the punishment when caught." It has stayed with me.

Moral knowledge founded upon values is the foundation of goodness in an individual. These values may be religious, cultural, or personal, but they provide a foundation upon which we can build our lives. One of my core values is procedural justice, which ensures that processes are just and equitable. It is not a legalistic justice, but rather an attempt to do good in each transaction. What is right is fairness, not so that I will be thanked, but because it is for the greater good. That belief causes me to view not just my occupation but also my ministry.

OVERCOMING SETBACKS

Setbacks have been an ongoing part of my life. Starting over is always daunting. It is like coming head-to-head with a monster you must learn to defeat. Stress weighs on you as a man, husband, father, brother, and son. Not only are you attempting to make a living, but you are also juggling multiple roles and responsibilities.

One significant setback came when I realized that career advancement isn't always about how qualified or hardworking you are. At Wells Fargo, I expected my master's degree and strong track record to lead to a promotion to senior vice president naturally. I saw people whom I had trained being promoted over me. It was a harsh reality that career progression often stems from doing your job well and doing that little extra.

For instance, when I was doing community volunteering and representing Wells Fargo, I was not aware that all that effort would ultimately define my professional path. Board service, non-profit work, and relationship building were not a part of my work, but they enabled me to acquire skill sets and networks that would open doors in the future.

Over the years, I have served on numerous boards, including the American Red Cross, the Iowa Asian Alliance, the Iowa Council for International Understanding (ICIU), and the Lutheran Church of Hope, now one of America's largest and most extensive rapidly expanding Lutheran churches.

Those experiences provided me with valuable exposure to leadership, teamwork, and community service. Interestingly, one of the non-profits I worked for as a community development officer, the Evelyn K Davis Center, is now an employer. Looking back, I now clearly understand that setbacks have shaped my life. What seemed like roadblocks turned out to be stepping stones to better opportunities.

THE SECOND HALF OF MY LIFE

As I reflect on my life, I see it as a game of two halves. Growth, challenges, and significant milestones marked the first half of my journey from zero to 60. I'm balancing ambition with a steady, measured approach in the second half. I've accumulated a great deal of mileage, both physically, emotionally, and spiritually.

This phase of my life is about applying everything I've learned from corporate roles, non-profit work, and leadership positions to serve others more intentionally. Am I perfect? Absolutely not. But the journey isn't over. I tell people, "We're not fixing the plane as it's flying. I aim to land it, repair it, and take off again." That's where I am in my career now: learning, growing, and preparing for the next flight.

Building a Family and Navigating Parenting in a New Culture

My wife and I began dating in 1989, and our relationship quickly developed into a strong and loving one. It was peaceful and built on trust, understanding, and a shared faith. Emily came from a strong Christian background; she grew up Anglican, and I grew up in a Catholic household. This shared foundation strengthened our bond, and we centered our friendship on mutual respect and love. We celebrated holidays like Christmas, Easter, and birthdays during our college years.

After I graduated, I traveled overseas to Ukraine for further opportunities, while Emily remained in Nigeria to complete her studies. Being a senior, I had already finished my program, but she still had more years to go. This meant our relationship became long-distance. In those days, there were no cell phones; we had only landlines at home, and I could only reach her during holidays when she was home. We relied on letters to communicate. I would write to her and mail the letters; if someone were traveling to Nigeria, I'd send notes and small gifts through them. It was challenging. Many people told her that I wouldn't return for her, that I would move on, and that she should do the same. But I'm a man of my word, and I meant it when I told her I'd marry her. Despite the challenges and doubts, we held on.

After over three years of a long-distance relationship, Emily graduated and completed her mandatory youth service. At this point, it was time to solidify our relationship. My family already knew her well. She had visited my home many times while I was still in Nigeria, and even after I left, she continued to visit my parents during her holidays. My siblings often visited her and fondly referred to her as "our big brother's wife," even though we weren't officially married yet.

In our Benin culture, marriage begins with an introduction. I sent a message to my family to initiate the process. As tradition dictates, the oldest man in my family met the eldest in Emily's family. In our culture, they symbolically describe the proposal as "Our son is interested in a flower in your compound." After identifying which "flower" they were referring to, the discussions and formalities began.

I returned to Nigeria from Ukraine to finalize all the

details. However, given the time constraints, I told my family we couldn't plan a whole wedding during my short trip. Instead, I promised we would hold the wedding in Ukraine, and Emily would join me there.

In 1997, Emily joined me in Ukraine, and we got married that same year. Interestingly, I chose September 28 as our wedding date, which also happens to be her birthday. I made this deliberate choice not because I wanted to save on gifts but because I thought it would be special to celebrate two milestones on the same day. Our wedding day became a double celebration, a beautiful union, and Emily's birthday.

It felt symbolic of the life we were starting together, full of meaning and shared moments. We got married at the Nazarene Church, and it was a celebration filled with love, happiness, and the joy of seeing a dream come true. However, life was different as a young couple living outside our home country. Without the familiar dynamics of an extended family around, we had to figure out everything about marriage traditions, challenges, and sweet moments on our own.

As newlyweds living in Ukraine, we quickly realized that building a life in a foreign land required resilience. We were eager to start a family immediately, but it wasn't forthcoming. This became a source of concern, and I later realized that Emily was struggling to adjust. She felt fearful and uneasy due to the crime and the unsettling things she had seen on TV and in our neighborhood. During this challenging time, we turned to prayer. We promised God that we would adopt one child if He blessed us with one, and if He blessed us with two, we would adopt two, creating a family of four. For a while, nothing happened, and we held on to our faith.

Two years later, we moved from Ukraine to Spain. Life as a young couple in a new country brought challenges as we tried to find our footing and figure out what the future held. During this time, Emily became pregnant with our first child. Around the same time was when I played the U.S. Diversity Visa Lottery and won by another stroke of luck.

Our first son, Enrique, was born in Spain in 1999. It was a moment of pure joy. In our tradition, the grandparents name the first grandchild. Overjoyed to welcome their first grandchild, my parents named him Edoghogho, which means "Day of Joy." His full name became Enrique Edoghogho, keeping with my promise that all our children's names would start with the letter "E."

Being a first-time father was intimidating but impressive. First-time mothering in a foreign place with no support from a family member was just as intimidating for Emily. New mothers in Africa are often surrounded by their families, mothers, aunts, and cousins, but for us, none were there. We had no one, no friends, no faces we had grown to recognize, just us navigating this new life together. We triumphed, energized by our love and shared goals. Meanwhile, the green card process took about two years, during which Emily became pregnant with our second child.

Our second son, Edward, was born in 2000 in Benin City, Nigeria, at the University of Benin Teaching Hospital (UBTH). We had traveled back to Nigeria as part of the green card process, which required us to attend an interview at the U.S. Consulate in Lagos. Edward was just two weeks old when we went for the interview. Despite the challenges of traveling with a newborn, we were granted visas for the entire family. As per tradition, my parents named him Edward Emwanta, keeping with the "E" theme. Emwanta means "Truth." With our green cards in hand, we boarded a plane and began our journey to the United States, settling in Des Moines, Iowa, on September 7, 2000.

Arriving in Iowa with two young children and no family around was yet another daunting chapter. We were just trying to learn how to live in a new country. But we approached the challenges with perseverance, steadfastness, and a focus on our dreams. We reminded ourselves that we had no children not long ago, and now we are blessed with two. Instead of complaining, we embraced this new reality as a blessing.

While trying to adjust to life in America, Emily became pregnant with our third child, Elliott. In 2001, we welcomed our third son into the world. His name was inspired by my former professor, Professor Elliott, who was head of the Quantity Surveying Department at Auchi Polytechnic and significantly influenced my education. My mother-in-law gave him his middle name, Edosa, meaning "Day of Joy," in keeping with the "E" theme.

With three children born in quick succession in 1999, 2000, and 2001, we were a growing family navigating life in a new land. It was challenging but fulfilling, and we were determined to build a strong foundation for our family, no matter the obstacles.

THE NAMING TRADITION AND RAISING CHILDREN

In our family, it's customary for the elders to give the children their traditional names, often used as middle names. This tradition continued with our children. We have Elliott Edosa, which means "Day of Joy," Edward Emwanta, and Enrique Edoghogho. All their names start with "E," just as I promised from the very beginning. That promise came to pass.

Initially, we prayed for two children, but God blessed us with three. This left us wondering how to fulfill our prayerful promise to adopt children in number to match the ones He blessed us with. Were we to adopt three children to fulfill our vow? That seemed unfeasible. After much discussion, we decided to support an existing orphanage instead. However, when I traveled to Nigeria in 2003 to explore this idea, I was heartbroken by what I saw. The state of the orphanages I visited was disheartening. That experience led us to start our orphanage, which gave birth to Cornerstone of Hope Orphanage.

BALANCING FAMILY, CAREER, AND EXTENDED RESPONSIBILITIES

Raising children in a foreign country without extended family support was not easy. At the same time, I was trying to build my career, be a supportive husband, and balance the responsibilities of being a son and a brother. As the first in my family to travel abroad, the expectations were heavy. My parents, siblings, and cousins relied on me for financial and emotional support.

There were many challenges, but my faith kept me grounded. I leaned heavily on a men's group at my church called Pretty Interesting Guys Stuff (P.I.G.S.), which became a powerhouse of support for me. This group of men, comprising grandfathers, retired professionals, and businessmen, became like brothers to me. We met each Thursday from 6:00 a.m. to 8:00 a.m., sharing wisdom, encouragement, and mutual accountability. This fellowship of believers shaped my mind and kept me centered in midlife.

Fatherhood in America was not something I was accustomed to. Raised in poverty, I was now living with my children in a country of abundance. It was hard to distinguish their wants from their needs and to recognize where to draw the boundary between too much and enough. Early on, I realized I was spoiling my kids because I didn't want them to experience the lack I grew up with.

However, I quickly learned the importance of teaching them the values of discipline and gratitude. My principle of enabling others also extends to my children. I believe in helping people succeed today rather than hoarding resources for the future, and this approach has shaped my parenting philosophy.

Discipline was another challenge. In Nigeria, we practiced spanking as a form of correction, but here, you talk and hope they listen. I learned that American kids can be stubborn and often insist they know better, even when they don't. Early childhood education significantly shaped my children's growth, teaching them leadership skills and independence, which were new to me.

PRESERVING MY CULTURE AND LANGUAGE

One of my biggest regrets is not teaching my children my native language, Edo, fluently. My wife and I initially tried to teach them when they were little. We would speak Edo to them, but they would respond, "Is that Spanish?" Confusion arose because Spanish was more prominent in their school environment, and they didn't hear Edo anywhere else. While they never became fluent in Edo, they understand it, mainly when it is used for correction. Hearing their parents speak it at home exposed them to their roots, but I wish I had done more to embed the language in their daily lives. Despite these challenges, raising my children has been one of the most fulfilling aspects of my life. Each child brought unique joy and purpose to our family. Although we may not have had extended family nearby, we built a close-knit household grounded in faith, love, and perseverance.

The lessons I learned as a father continue to guide me in all aspects of life, reinforcing the importance of family and culture and the promise to always do my best for those I love.

RAISING MULTICULTURAL CHILDREN IN AMERICA

When my boys misbehaved, especially in public places like Walmart, I would switch to speaking my native language, Edo. I'd say something like, "U gha rhie ikan." This phrase means that if you do not behave, you will be disciplined. The moment they heard it, they'd straighten up. Curious about what I said, my American friends would ask, "What does that mean?" I'd jokingly reply, "I told them I'd give them flowers." Of course, I couldn't openly explain the real meaning in public.

While my children learned a few corrective phrases in Edo, they never became fluent, which is one of my biggest regrets. They bear the name Idehen, and people often ask, "Where does your last name come from?" They proudly answer, "Nigeria," but they don't speak any Nigerian languages.

This missed opportunity weighs on me because language is vital to cultural identity. When my wife and I were little, we initially tried to teach them Edo, but they often confused it with Spanish, a language they frequently heard at school. Over time, we stopped speaking Edo at home consistently. During my years abroad, juggling multiple languages made it challenging to focus on just one.

THE JOY OF SOCCER AND TRANSFERABLE SKILLS

One thing I did well as a father was introducing my boys to soccer. Growing up in Nigeria, I played soccer barefoot. My knees were often scraped and bleeding from falls on rough, rocky fields, but it didn't stop me from loving the game. When I saw my boys playing in their cleats, shin guards, and comfortable socks, I often joked, "How can you not excel with all this protection? We didn't even have shoes!"

When they were young, I took them to the field and taught them what we called "street soccer." These were learnable only through playing spontaneously, but were readily adapted to organized play. Soccer isn't merely a matter of kicking the ball; it also involves strategy, leadership, and accuracy. I taught them to play with a purpose, understand their opponents' weaknesses and strengths, and anticipate exactly where to kick the ball ahead of time.

All three boys became skilled players. Our oldest played

soccer in college, and during one memorable high school season, all three played varsity together as a junior, freshman, and senior at Urbandale High School. It was a point of pride for us to have "Idehen" at the top of the field three at a time. Individuals would approach us after a match and inquire about their performance, and it was at such times that we confirmed their training had paid off.

INSTILLING THE LESSONS OF DISCIPLINE AND HEALTHY HABITS IN OUR CHILDREN

Discipline wasn't just about behavior; it also extended to their eating habits. Growing up in Nigeria, I didn't have access to candies or sugary treats, so I didn't feel the need to introduce those things to my kids. Candy was a rarity in our home, only appearing during Halloween or as occasional treats from school or birthday parties.

Similarly, soda was not commonly found in our household. We consumed juice and water. This lack of sugar has affected the children's cravings; to this day, they remain uninterested in sweets or soda. Cake is only spoken of on birthdays or special occasions. This approach to food was not only about health.. It was also about balance and not giving in to excess.

ADOPTION AND THE DESIRE FOR A DAUGHTER

In 2013, my wife and I began discussing adoption more seriously. As parents of three boys, we often talked about wanting a daughter. Growing up in a family of seven boys and one sister, I didn't want to repeat the same dynamic of overwhelming male energy. Since we didn't seem able to "make one" naturally, we decided to explore adoption.

We had this little child named Divine at our orphanage in Nigeria. We believed that was our awaited-for daughter, but the process of adopting her did not go according to our wishes due to some issues. Unfortunately, things did not work out, and we were unable to adopt her.

Despite such disappointment, our visit strengthened our resolve to help orphans and vulnerable children. It also reminded us of the promise we made before God to care for needy children by adopting them.. Even though we did not adopt a daughter, our encounter with the orphanage has blessed us with endless blessings that have filled our lives with contentment, allowing us to be part of something greater than ourselves.

Parenting has been one of the richest and most humbling experiences of my life. From soccer practices to modeling values and good habits, I've poured everything I could into preparing them for a world that holds promise but also peril. While I have regrets, such as being unable to instruct them in my language, I take pride in what I've taught them and the family we've built together.

As a dad, I now understand that perfection is not an accomplishment; rather, it is a combination of persistence, love, and a commitment to doing one's best for one's children and family. It is not done, and I look forward to seeing what happens next with our family and our future together.

THE JOURNEY TO EXPANDING OUR FAMILY

When my wife and I discussed adopting, our perspectives initially clashed. She wanted a baby she could bond with and nurture from the start, but I was adamant I was done with diapers. At the time, our boys were one, two, and three years old, and I was practically a regular at Walmart. The employees could tell immediately why I was there and would direct me straight to the diaper aisle. The idea of starting over with a baby felt overwhelming.

"I want a child at least four years old," I told her. But we couldn't agree on a date, so we put the idea on hold. Later, when an adoption from our orphanage didn't work out, the situation forced a difficult conversation. A little girl named Divine had been preparing to join a family in the U.S., but the process fell through. Someone needed to break the news to her. I initially refused. "I can't be the one to break her heart," I said.

Eventually, I agreed on one condition: I would deliver

both good and bad news. "What's the good news?" my wife asked. I responded, "We'll adopt her ourselves." My wife teased me, "Now you're just trying to get what you want: an older child." But deep down, I couldn't bear to leave Divine feeling abandoned. I've always believed in carrying positive energy, not negativity. After much discussion, my wife agreed, and we began the adoption process.

WELCOMING DIVINE

After almost 17 months of navigating the complex adoption process, Divine officially joined our family. When she moved in, she was eight years old and quickly became the light of our home. Today, she's 17, attending Urbandale High School, and thriving. She is graduating from High School this summer.

When she arrived, we discussed changing her name to fit our "E Family" tradition. Even my car's license plate read "E Family." I suggested she could be called Evine, removing the "D" from her name. But Divine was firm. "I want to keep my name," she said, and we respected her choice.

As is our tradition with the orphanage, all children receive my father's middle name, Edokpaigbe, which means "May this child live and thrive." Divine adopted our last name despite not conforming to our traditional "E" naming policy. She brought new energy to the home, and we all gained from her.

LEARNING TO RAISE A DAUGHTER

Having raised three boys, I thought I had this parenting thing figured out. But Divine taught me differently. She introduced me to the world of pink and purple. I remember one shopping trip when I tried to buy just one color of something, and she looked at me with such determination that I didn't even realize it when I pulled out my credit card to buy both.

Her transition to our home wasn't without its quirks. Coming from the orphanage, where survival meant hiding your belongings to keep them safe, Divine would stash food and other items under her bed. It took time for her to understand that nothing would be taken away from her here.

By fifth grade, she had adjusted well to her new life, and by the time she reached seventh and eighth grade, she had developed an American accent. Now, she even corrects my English! "That's not how you pronounce it, Dad," she'll say. It's amusing and heartwarming at the same time.

DIVINE'S IMPACT

Divine brought a sense of balance and new energy to our home. She's the family's entrepreneur, a natural leader who keeps everyone in line. At just 17, she has already paid off her car despite working part-time. She is also an outstanding student and a source of pride for us. It has been a dream come true to have Divine in our lives. Her growth from an orphanage child to a confident, vibrant young lady is a living testament to the power of opportunity combined with love. Divine's life is intertwined with our dream for the orphanage.

We intend to take these "rejected stones" and shape them into "cornerstones" of people who will mature, make a difference in the world, and minister to others. Divine embodies that vision. She is a cornerstone in our family, reminding us daily of the beauty of resilience and the importance of giving every child a chance to thrive.

BEING GUIDED BY FAITH, GRATITUDE, AND FAMILY TRADITIONS

The world becomes better when we embrace love and serve others selflessly. Let us create a world without the divide between the "haves" and "have-nots," without envy, jealousy, or hatred, one that thrives on love.

When people thank me for starting the orphanage, I humbly say, "No. Thank the children for letting me serve God through them. This fulfills my contract with God." That sense of purpose shapes everything I do as a father, husband, and community member.

Faith is the cornerstone of our family. We celebrate Christmas, Easter, and other Christian traditions with gratitude and joy. For us, these aren't just events; they are reminders to live a life of service and love for others. We teach our children to give thanks to God in every situation. It's not just about physically attending church, though it is part of it. Even if you can't attend in person, we encourage you to participate in online services or moments of personal reflection.

The first thing we emphasize is gratitude for waking up each day. "You didn't wake up by your power," I often tell them. "It is by God's grace." I remind them of this humorously, saying, "If you think your alarm clock wakes you up, try setting one at the mortuary and see if it wakes the dead." That lesson has become part of our family lore, and my children understand that every breath we take is a gift from God.

CELEBRATING MILESTONES AND ACHIEVEMENTS IN OUR HOME

We believe in celebrating achievements, big or small. Birthdays are special, but so are graduations and other educational milestones. Each of our boys had the same celebratory acknowledgment when they graduated from high school and college, and we're excited to do the same for Divine, who is now a senior in high school.

Our youngest, Elliot, is now a junior in college, and we are just as proud of him. We celebrate these milestones with our family, reminisce about all that went into reaching each accomplishment, and share in the celebration together. Our celebrations don't stop with our immediate family. We also celebrate with our extended family members and friends. We attend our friends' graduation ceremonies just like we do our own. We assist each other in every way possible.

THE "E FAMILY GOVERNMENT"

In our home, we refer to it as the "E Family Government." We make major, or sometimes small, decisions together. We all sit together, discuss the matter, and take our vote. If there are more "yeses" than "nays," we go for it. It is based on collaboration and equity, instilling in our children the practice of consensus and collective responsibility.

ADOPTING AND HONORING TRADITIONS

Being in America has introduced us to various traditions, such as Thanksgiving and Independence Day. Even though we wish each day were Thanksgiving Day, we enjoy such holidays to reflect upon past times and reunite. We take our cultural traditions with us on our journey through life. They have brought our family together and our feet close to the ground, from our milestone celebrations to instilling a sense of gratitude and belonging in us.

Over time, our traditions have evolved, but our spirit remains unchanged: love, faith, and gratitude. Whether for birthdays, anniversaries, or simply because we're thankful for waking up every morning, these are reminders of the blessings we enjoy. One of our highlights was that our boys traveled to Europe to play soccer. Enrique, Edward, and Elliott embarked on trips that placed their ability in the spotlight and tested their strength of character and independence.

At the age of 11, he was fortunate enough to travel to Austria and Germany through the People-to-People program. Spain's Leganés even gave him a trial, which was a dream come true for a player at such an early stage of his development. Elliott and Edward were able to train with England's West Ham Academy under one of their sub-coaches. At 18 and 19, respectively, they went to Las Palmas, Spain, to play soccer with a local club and to train.

Elliott finished high school studies at the American International School of Las Palmas, graduating from the demanding school and football calendars. They spent two years overseas, juggling their calendars, attending school after football training, and navigating language difficulties. It gave our boys grit, adaptability, resilience, and perseverance.

INDEPENDENCE AND DEVELOPMENT

It was thrilling and daunting for Emily and me to watch our boys fighting it out at such a tender age. It brought to mind traveling in America, Spain, and Ukraine. I could identify resonance with what I had lived through in them: learning, succeeding on my own, and flourishing under adversity. Their exposure was not just to football; it was also about maturity and learning to cope with the sophistication of living abroad. Their role is one that I, their father, am glad they fulfilled. Their ability to enjoy life is a virtue that enabled me to believe in their ability to try any adventure possible.

Those adventures helped shape them into confident, capable young men. For us parents, it was an absolute pleasure to see them grow up and chase their dreams, gaining life skills that would last for many years to come. Being raised in a traditional, religious family is an honor and a delight. It reminds us that we can endure trials with perseverance, steadfastness, and love, and celebrate every blessing that comes our way.

Founding the Nonprofit

The Birth of Cornerstone of Hope Orphanage

The inspiration and motivation behind Cornerstone of Hope Orphanage were born from two defining moments in my life, one profoundly personal and the other rooted in a profound realization about the state of orphans in Nigeria. When my wife and I married, we were eager to start a family. We imagined the joy of welcoming our first child, watching them grow, and experiencing the incredible gift of parenthood. But things didn't go as planned. Month after month, year after year, nothing happened. The waiting turned into anxiety, then frustration, and eventually, surrender. One night, my wife and I prayed in our most vulnerable moment.

We pledged before God that if He granted us children of our own, we would take in children in need and offer them love, care, and chances that were their due. Shortly after that, our prayers were granted. We were blessed with three wonderful sons, Enrique, Edward, and Elliot, within a span of three years. It was a miracle, a humility-inducing show of faith. But even with our growing family, our promise never left my heart. I couldn't shake the thought of the millions of children around the world, especially in my home country, Nigeria, who had no parents, no stable home, and no future.

I knew it wasn't enough to be grateful for what we had; we had to act on our promise and extend the same love to those in need. Initially, we had considered partnering with orphanages in Nigeria. Still, every home we visited came with a heartbreaking reality that we couldn't, in good faith, give our resources to homes where children were often neglected. That is how Cornerstone of Hope Orphanage was born.

THE REJECTED STONE BECOMING THE CORNERSTONE

As I prayed about the orphanage, I kept returning to a scripture that spoke directly to my spirit: *"The stone the builders rejected has become the cornerstone; the Lord has done this, and it is marvelous in our eyes." – Matthew 21:42*

This verse resonated deeply with me. I thought about orphans, the forgotten children of society, rejected, abandoned, and discarded. If we could take those children, nurture them, and pour into their lives, they could become cornerstones, strong, valuable individuals who could one day transform the world. This became the mission and heartbeat of Cornerstone of Hope Orphanage:

- To rescue and restore orphaned and abandoned children.
- To provide a nurturing, faith-filled environment where they can heal and grow.
- To equip them with education and life skills to build their own future.
- To instill in them a heart of service so they, too, can uplift others.

It wasn't just about housing children; it was about providing them with a safe and nurturing environment. It was about empowering them to rewrite their stories and become leaders who would change the narrative for generations to come.

The Cornerstone of Hope Orphanage's beginnings are deeply rooted in biblical scripture, particularly in the parable of the stone that was rejected but became a cornerstone. Not only did this scripture, Matthew 21:42, inspire the orphanage's name, but it also gave direction to its mission, philosophy, and unwavering commitment to transforming lives. For many, this verse is simply a metaphor, representing Jesus' rejection by mankind and His ultimate role as the foundation of faith. However, for the children of Cornerstone of Hope and I, this verse is more than just a theological concept; it is a living, breathing reality.

The cornerstone is the first stone set in the construction of a building. It serves as the foundation upon which the entire structure rests. In biblical times, builders would sometimes reject stones that appeared flawed, weak, or unfit for use. Yet, in this parable, the stone cast aside by the world became the most critical and foundational part of the structure.

When I think about orphans, children who have been abandoned, cast away, or deemed unworthy by society, I see the same story unfolding. Through no fault of their own, these children have been rejected by the world. Some have been left at hospital gates, others at church doors, and some at the very gate of the orphanage. They are often seen as burdens, as children who are too difficult to care for or as those who may never amount to anything.

But God's plan is different.
- *What society rejects, God redeems.*
- *What the world casts away, God elevates.*
- *What seems broken, God restores.*

The children who enter Cornerstone of Hope are not just orphans in need of charity; they are chosen vessels of God's grace. They are meant to be more than their circumstances, more than their past, and more than what the world has told them they are. They are destined to be leaders, change-makers, and examples of God's transformative power.

When I first heard the call to start an orphanage, I did not realize how this scripture would be applied to my ministry. I was only concerned with establishing a warm, safe home where these children could reside, eat, sleep, and attend school. But over the years, I realized that Cornerstone of Hope was not called to be an asylum but a cornerstone. It was not just caring for orphans but a process of building leaders who in turn, could lead others. It was revealed that my role was not just about helping these children survive, but also about helping them thrive.

This was a missioin of equipping them with tools, resources, and affirmation to unleash their potential. This was mission to remind them each day: *You are not an orphan; you are a Cornerstone.* It changed everything for the children. Life wasn't easy for any child that comes to the home. Many come with deep emotional wounds. Some have been abused, others neglected. Many arrive skeptical, not knowing whether this home will be any different from the places that abandoned them before. Healing takes time.

At Cornerstone, we prioritize restoration, not just survival. Each child is given the space to heal, grow, and begin to see themselves as more than just victims of their past. Many of our children struggle with abandonment trauma. They often ask, "Why me? Why didn't my parents want me? Am I not good enough?" We work with counselors, caregivers, and volunteers who help them unlearn rejection and embrace self-worth. Education is the bridge between rejection and transformation. By providing every child with education, we empower them to break the cycle of poverty. Education is their key to freedom, and we help them realize it. Here, we don't just talk about faith; we practice it. We are showing children God's unwavering love and their ability to move mountains with faith. They understand that humans may have lost faith in them, but not in God.

Besides education, we prepare our children for adulthood by equipping them with vocational skills, leadership programs, and, most importantly, values of integrity, hard work, and service. Perhaps one of the most rewarding parts of the journey is seeing mature adults who were former orphans return to serve. Some children who grew up at the orphanage return later as volunteers, mentors, and sponsors.

One young man, who once thought he was abandoned for life, now runs a business that helps other struggling youth. A young woman who once thought no one wanted her now works as a social worker, helping children in crisis. These are not just feel-good stories. They are living testimonies of what God can do when we refuse to let rejection define us.

The work is far from over. For every child we have been able to uplift, countless more are still waiting. For every orphan who has found a home, there are others who remain lost. For every rejected stone that has become a cornerstone, many more are waiting to be discovered, nurtured, and elevated.

This mission is bigger than just one orphanage, one country, or one moment in time. It is a global calling, a movement to ensure that no child is ever left behind because of the circumstances of their birth.

We must all ask ourselves:
"Who are the rejected stones around me?"
"How can I help them become cornerstones?"
Whether through mentorship, sponsorship, donations, or simply extending kindness to someone in need, we all have a role to play. God is still in the business of turning rejection into redemption. As long as Cornerstone of Hope stands, we will continue to be the hands and feet of that transformation.

THE CHALLENGES OF BUILDING THE CORNERSTONE OF HOPE

Starting from scratch was challenging; I had a vision, but I lacked the resources to bring it to life. My wife and I committed our plans and vision to God, believing He would make it happen in His way and in His time. When I first shared my vision with others, many thought I was crazy. I was then a bank teller, barely making ends meet, and my wife was a stay-at-home mom with our three small boys. We were scraping by on our own. I recall discussing this with a mentor and receiving reassurance.

What he told me was: "Eric, take care of your own family first. You don't even have enough for yourself. How could you possibly take care of other people's children?" He was well-meaning but did not succeed in discouraging me. I could view the resources from a human perspective, considering costs and determining what was needed. But I viewed them from God's perspective, trusting in God's provision rather than mine.

He meant well, but his words didn't deter me. I knew he was evaluating things from a human perspective, calculating resources, and counting costs. But I was evaluating them from a divine perspective, trusting in God's provision rather than my own.

I started with what I had; I gathered a committee of trusted friends in Nigeria and the U.S. to serve as board members. I registered the orphanage as a 501(c)(3) nonprofit organization in the United States and as a non-governmental organization (NGO) in Nigeria. I decided to use my childhood home as the first site for the orphanage. I demolished and rebuilt it into a multi-story facility that could house up to 50 children.

Though we had space for 50, we never housed that many at once. Instead, we maintained a manageable number between 19 and 26, allowing us to give each child personalized care and attention.

NAVIGATING GOVERNMENT BUREAUCRACY IN NIGERIA

One of the most complex challenges was dealing with the Nigerian government. Even though we were helping orphaned children, government officials still expected bribes to process the paperwork. They called it "appreciation," but I called it corruption. When I refused to pay, my paperwork was delayed for months. The longer I stayed in Nigeria to handle these matters, the more money I lost, and the more my work in the U.S. was affected. But I refused to compromise my values. Eventually, we succeeded in obtaining complete registration, and Cornerstone of Hope became recognized as one of the top orphanages in Edo State.

Running a nonprofit in Nigeria, especially an orphanage, is not just about providing food, shelter, and education; it is also about fostering a sense of community and belonging. It is also a relentless battle against bureaucracy, inefficiency, and corruption. Every step, from registration to daily operations, is tangled in red tape designed to frustrate, delay, and ultimately force compliance with an unspoken system of bribery and extortion.

When Cornerstone of Hope Orphanage was in its initial stages of development, it was conceived with a commitment, a faith promise. It would be a haven, a sanctuary for homeless children, where they could find love, education, and a future. I did not anticipate the complexity of dealing with government agencies, the institutions that should have been partners in our mission, but instead became obstacles.

The first hurdle was registration. To be recognized as

a legal entity, we had to go through the Corporate Affairs Commission in Abuja, obtain approval from the Ministry of Women Affairs and Social Development, and register with local and state governments. It should have been a straightforward process. I gathered all the necessary documents, completed the required forms, and approached the relevant offices with the confidence of someone who believed that following the law should be sufficient. It was not.

There was a reason for each step's delay: some documents required authentication, some signatures needed to be processed, or some authorizations took time to complete. Not long before, it was apparent that these were not obstacles but coded messages. If you wanted things to go faster, you had to say thank you. I distinctly remember one trip to a government office in Benin City. He scanned through my documents, nodded wordlessly, and leaned back in his chair.

"Oga, everything looks good," he said, tapping the file on his desk. *"But you know how we do things here."*

I knew what he meant, but I refused to play along.

"What do you mean?" I asked.

"You need to appreciate the office."

"For what?"

"For our time," he said, shrugging.

The meaning was clear. No matter how perfect my documents were, nothing would move forward unless I "motivated" the system. When I refused, my paperwork mysteriously disappeared, resurfacing months after repeated visits and escalating frustration. Eventually, we received our registration without paying a bribe, but it took nearly twice as long as it should have. I later learned that other orphanages had completed their registrations in half the time by simply "appreciating" the right people.

Once the orphanage was legally established, the battle was far from over. We were required to renew our license with the Ministry of Women's Affairs annually, which involved filing reports, undergoing inspections, and providing financial statements. Again, it should have been routine but it was not.

When government inspectors arrived, their focus was rarely on the well-being of the children. Instead, they searched for any minor infraction that could be used as leverage. Something as simple as a missing signature in a report could be blown out of proportion into a serious compliance issue unless we are willing to address it informally. One inspector pulled my supervisor aside and said, *"If you don't settle with us, we will write a report stating that your orphanage is unfit."*

This was the system we were up against. Instead of supporting those genuinely working to improve the lives of vulnerable children, government agencies treated orphanages as revenue streams, extracting money rather than partnering in a shared mission to support them. Perhaps the most heartbreaking aspect of dealing with the bureaucracy was the adoption process. When a child is abandoned or orphaned, the Ministry of Women's Affairs places them in an approved orphanage. However, when families come forward to adopt, we, the people who have cared for these children, nurtured them, and watched them grow, are entirely excluded from the decision-making process.

The government controls all adoptions, and orphanages cannot vet or even meet the adopting families. We received a call from the ministry instructing us to bring a specific child to their office. That is the last time we see them. The strict policies that do not allow orphanages to have any direct contact with adopting families break my heart. We receive no details about the adopters, no updates, and no way to ensure the child is going to a safe and loving home.

We might raise a child from infancy to two years old, bonding with them, nurturing them, and then suddenly, we receive a call: "Bring Baby Michael to the Ministry at 10 a.m. tomorrow." Just like that, the child is gone. No goodbye, no follow-up, and no assurance that they are in good hands. For babies, this process is more straightforward. But it is heartbreaking for older children, those who have spent years in our care, calling us "Mommy" and "Daddy" and seeing the other children as siblings.

One of the most challenging cases involved a three-year-old girl named Bella. She had been with us since she was a baby and had formed a deep bond with one of our nannies, whom she affectionately called "Mama." When the ministry informed us that she had been adopted, we had no choice but to dress her in her best clothes, packed her belongings, and took her to the ministry's office. There was no transition, no preparation. One moment, she was in a place she knew as home, and the next, she was being handed over to strangers. We never heard from her again.

It felt like a loss, a kind of death, and yet we had no closure. We did not know if she was safe, if she was loved, if she would ever remember the people who had cared for her. The system did not allow us to ask. I pleaded with the ministry to introduce a process that would enable orphanages to remain in contact with adopted children, even if only for an annual update. The answer was a firm no.

"If the families know you, they might feel pressured to send money or stay connected, which could cause problems." They said. That was the official explanation. The truth was likely far more complex. Transparency was not in their interest. Despite all these challenges, the government did not fund orphanages. We received no financial assistance, provisions, or medical support. Yet, the government expected us to care for these children indefinitely, and when it was time for them to be adopted, we were not even allowed to know where they

were going.

During the holiday season, an official called and casually asked, *"Oga, it's the end of the year, send something small for us."*

"You want me to send you money for Christmas," I said, *"when I have twenty children here who need Christmas clothes, food, and gifts?"*

He laughed as if I had made a joke. *"You know how it is,"* he said.

This is what is happening with the Nigerian bureaucracy. The same system that should be fighting to protect and help children is often one of the most significant hurdles to their well-being. Through all these disappointments, however, I will not yield. At Cornerstone of Hope Orphanage, we are committed to transparency and integrity, and a system that works for the children it is intended to assist. We are working to build a future where orphans are not treated as commodities, adoption is rooted in care and responsibility, and those who dedicate their lives to helping others are not punished for their integrity. It's a long way, but we will continue with it because these children, these so-called discarded stones, deserve to become cornerstones of something better.

PATRICK'S JOURNEY OF TRIUMPH

Patrick's story is one of hope, strength, and survival; he was brought to the Cornerstone of Hope Orphanage with his sisters,

Favour and Antonia. Patrick and his siblings had a sorrowful past, one of loss and adversity. There were not three more children in need of a home to lay their heads when brought to the orphanage; they were three shattered souls in need of love, stability, and hope for a future hitherto unimaginable to them. Patrick, being the oldest, carried an unspoken burden. Even at a tender age, he became the guardian, insulating his siblings from the trauma of orphaning.

He was quiet but observant, always watching, always trying to figure out how things worked. His eyes carried the weight of someone who had seen too much, who had been forced to grow up too soon. We provided food, shelter, and education at the orphanage, but the most important thing we could offer was a sense of family. Patrick, however, struggled to accept it.

He had been let down too often before, and trust did not come easily. He kept his guard up, never fully allowing himself to believe that this place, this new reality, was truly home. Over the years, his siblings found homes outside the orphanage. A Nigerian woman lovingly adopted Antonia, and an American family adopted Favour. Patrick was not so fortunate, however. He was left behind. Growing up, he began asking himself, *"Why hadn't anyone adopted me?"* Was he not good enough? Was there something wrong with him?

Helplessly, I saw the self-doubt creep in. He started

testing us by pulling away and acting increasingly rebellious. He was also testing us, pushing limits to learn if we would lose hope in him. I could recognize that this was his way of coping and protecting himself from rejection. My suspicions about his behavior were confirmed by Emily Crist, an 18-year-old American from Ohio, when she visited the Cornerstone of Hope Orphanage. Emily discovered that Patrick was not happy.

As a teenager, she could get words out of Patrick enough to change everything for good. Emily is now married and a mother of two beautiful sons. Emily and her family now live in Norway. One evening, after another difficult day of discipline and frustration, I sat him down for a talk. I told him something that I knew he might not believe at first.

"Patrick, your worth is not determined by whether someone adopts you or not; you are already chosen by God. You are chosen by the people here who love you. And you have the power to create your own future." He nodded, but his eyes were clouded with doubt. I knew words alone would not be enough. He needed something to hold on to, something tangible to work towards. So, I made him a promise.

"If you focus on your education, give it everything you have, and prove that you are ready to succeed, I will send you abroad for college. I don't know how, but I will make it happen." It was an ambitious pledge for which I didn't have a ready design, but I knew that Patrick had to hear it. He had

to understand that someone believed in him enough to invest in his future.

It was that conversation that changed everything. Patrick immersed himself in books, reading more than he had before. He no longer considered himself one left behind, but started to view himself as a man with a purpose. He excelled in school, consistently achieving top marks and grades and pleasing his teachers. He was smitten with numbers, and before long, he was sure he was suited to be an accountant.

By the time he completed high school, he was no longer that boy. He had become a driven individual, ready to take over the world. He stood before me with his grades, his head held high, his eyes shining with pride and expectation. *"Daddy, you promised,"* he said simply. And I had.

Finding a way to send Patrick abroad for his education was no small task. The United States and Canada were complicated options due to visa restrictions and financial constraints, which made many schools unattainable for many students. But then, an opportunity arose in the United Kingdom. De Montfort University in Leicester, UK, offered him admission to study accounting.

It was a moment of triumph but also one of challenge. We had to cover his fees, travel expenses, and accommodation. It was daunting, but we couldn't let this chance pass. We accomplished this with the help of donors, friends, and benefactors who believed in Patrick's promise. It was a day of conflicting thoughts. His fellow orphans stood by, looking on at their elder brother, their role model, as he prepared to embark on an adventure that had once been considered impossible. It was a joyful day, but it was also a sad day. Patrick inspired many of them, a living example that their destinies could be achieved.

Life in the UK was not without its struggles. Patrick had to adjust to a new culture, a different educational system, and the reality of being alone in a foreign land. But he faced these challenges with resilience and determination, as he had faced every obstacle before. He graduated with an accounting degree, indicating to himself and everyone else that his past did not define him. He had constructed his future and earned his way, but he was not done.

Upon his return from his studies, Patrick returned to Nigeria with a clear mission. He did not want to work for anyone else but to establish something for himself. He had seen firsthand the struggle of food scarcity and the struggle of sustaining oneself and understood that farming was a venture that could transform lives. He then established a poultry farm in Ogun State to make a positive impact.

It was not business to him, but empowerment. He had to generate jobs and food security, and prove to everyone else that there was no need to wait for things to be handed over to them. They could do it for themselves. Patrick's growth from an abandoned child to an educated businessman proves that what can be achieved is possible if you are given an opportunity and never lose hope. His story is not unique. It is a beacon of hope for every child at Cornerstone of Hope Orphanage.

Whenever I spoke to him, I recall the moment he stood before me and asked if I would keep my promise. Now, he is making promises to himself, his community, and the next generation of young people who will look at him and say, *"If Patrick could do it, so can I."*

His success is not just a personal achievement but a ripple effect. It is proof that the rejected stones can indeed become the cornerstone. It embodies the vision that built Cornerstone of Hope to share love, build hope, and change lives. Patrick's journey is far from over. But wherever it takes him next, one thing is sure: He will never again doubt his worth. He was never unwanted; he was always chosen.

THE CHOSEN ONES

At the heart of Cornerstone of Hope Orphanage are the children whose lives have been forever changed by the power of love, faith, and opportunity. Among them are six high school teenagers navigating their way through education, self-discovery, and the dreams they dare to dream. Life has not been easy for these six young individuals. They have experienced struggle, uncertainty, and the harsh realities of being without a stable family structure. But at Cornerstone, they have found more than just a place to sleep and food to eat. They have found a home, a family, and a future.

I never promised them the luxury of overseas education. Still, I did promise them something just as valuable: the opportunity to receive a high-quality education in Nigeria, one that would equip them with the knowledge and skills to build the lives they deserve. I have always believed that education is one of the greatest equalizers in life. With the proper education, they can break cycles of poverty, create opportunities for themselves, and ultimately pay it forward by helping others who once stood in their shoes.

I tell them daily that they are not orphans but the chosen ones. They are chosen by God to be blessed, lifted, and transformed into leaders of tomorrow. The minute they walk into the compound of Cornerstone of Hope, they are no longer victims of their circumstances. They are survivors, overcomers, and vessels of God's grace.

Every day, I see them waking up early, putting on their school uniforms, and heading out purposefully. They take their education seriously because they understand the importance of what is at stake. They know that this opportunity is their gateway to a brighter future. They study hard, excel in their subjects, and engage in extracurricular activities that shape their leadership abilities. One wishes to be a doctor, driven by the compassion of health workers who have cared for her over the years. Another wishes to be an engineer, eager to watch the development of buildings and infrastructure. One of the boys aspires to become a lawyer, driven by a desire to defend the voiceless. Each of them has their way, a dream that surpasses what exists; they do not wish to survive but to thrive.

However, providing a good education does not just involve paying school fees; it also requires a commitment to quality education. It means ensuring they can access school supplies, books, proper clothing, and, when needed, additional tutoring. It means creating an environment where they can focus on learning without worrying about their next meal or whether they will have a safe place to sleep at night.

FAITH, COMMUNITY, AND THE POWER OF SUPPORT

Running an orphanage was never part of my initial life plan. If someone had told me years ago that I would one day be responsible for the well-being of dozens of children, I would have laughed. But God's plan is often greater than our understanding, and He equips those He calls.

When I first started Cornerstone of Hope, I had no external funding. I had no big donors or corporate sponsorships. I had only a vision and an unwavering belief that if God had given me this mission, He would also provide the means to fulfill it.

I used my credit card to cover early school fees, food, clothing, and medical care expenses. It was not the most sustainable approach, but it was all I had in those first few years. And I refused to let financial challenges deter me from my calling. Over the years, God sent help in ways I could never have imagined. One of the greatest sources of support has been the Lutheran Church of Hope in West Des Moines, Iowa.

The members of this church, people who barely knew me at first, became a crucial part of the orphanage's success; people like Keith & Eileen Dener, Kevin & Phoelisa McGuire, Pam Avaux, Jim Adams, Pastor Jeremy Johnson, members of my men's group called Pretty Interesting Guys Stuff (P.I.G.S), etc. Their generosity, belief in our mission, and unwavering support have enabled us to continue growing and reaching more children. I am reminded of how kindness and belief transform people every time I am in church.

Some of these individuals have never traveled to Nigeria, but they donate generously to care for children that they have never met. They donate money, clothing, school supplies, and prayer. They do this not expecting praise but because their hearts are convinced of goodness and kindness. Apart from church life, my men's fellowship has been a source of strength. This fellowship of devoted men with long-standing experience in God's word has been with me since 2005.

They are my brothers, my advisors, and my friends. They

have offered guidance during difficult moments, helped with fundraising, and repeatedly reminded me that I am not alone in this journey. I often tell people that Cornerstone of Hope is my work and a community effort. It is the work of everyone who has ever contributed, prayed, or simply believed in the children we serve. It is the work of every teacher who has taught them, every volunteer who has spent time with them, and every sponsor who has made their education possible.

As these six teenagers prepare to graduate from high school in the coming years, I see endless possibilities ahead of them. They will have the opportunity to attend universities and vocational schools, or pursue careers that enable them to give back to society. But beyond their successes, my greatest hope is that they carry forward the spirit of Cornerstone. They remember where they came from and use their achievements to uplift others.

I pray that one day, these teens will mentor younger children, support orphanages, or even start initiatives to help the next generation. This is how we create lasting change. This is how we break cycles of poverty and despair. It is not just about providing a meal for today but about building a future where these children no longer need charity and become the givers, leaders, and inspirations. That is the true vision of Cornerstone of Hope.

As long as God gives me strength, I will continue to fight

for them, believe in them, and remind them daily that they are not orphans but the chosen ones.

MY PERSONAL PHILOSOPHY AND LEADERSHIP STYLE

The guiding principle of my life is deeply rooted in my faith. I believe in treating people with genuine love without expecting anything in return. This selfless approach is a moral code and a biblical mandate. When I reflect on the life and ministry of Jesus Christ, I see a man who led by example; He was simple, humble, and compassionate. He was not arrogant, nor did He seek recognition. Instead, He chose the back of the room, allowing others to be honored first. His humility and servant leadership shaped my own beliefs about how to live and lead.

Doing good should not be transactional; instead, it should benefit humanity as a whole. Too often, people perform good deeds with the expectation of reciprocation, but true service is given freely, expecting nothing in return. This belief influences how I navigate my personal life and my work.

Many people attribute success solely to hard work, but I see it differently. Yes, I work hard, but I also acknowledge the role of divine placement. I believe God gives opportunity, while preparedness results from diligence and effort. No matter how prepared a person is, success remains elusive if the chance is absent. My own life is a testimony to this. Winning the U.S. Green Card lottery was not something I orchestrated. It was a divine favor. If success were simply about effort, then I should have also won the Powerball, but to date, the most I have ever won is twelve dollars. This realization keeps me grounded in my faith, understanding that grace is pivotal in our journeys.

LEADERSHIP AND SERVANT MENTALITY

Humility is at the forefront of my leadership style and service to others. Jesus, the ultimate leader, washed the feet of his disciples, a powerful act of humility and service. Today, few leaders exhibit this kind of selflessness. Most acts of service by those in high positions are staged for publicity, but true servant leadership is a daily practice, not a performance.

I do not call myself a leader unless the word "servant" precedes it. True leadership is not about authority but about responsibility. I believe in transformational leadership, taking individuals, nurturing them, and guiding them toward their full potential. This belief stems from my childhood experiences, where creativity and resourcefulness were essential. We did not have store-bought toys; we made our own. We transformed scraps into treasures. That mindset shaped me into a leader who sees potential in people, even when they do not see it in themselves. I tell the children at Cornerstone of Hope Orphanage that they are not orphans but chosen ones. Society may label them based on their circumstances, but I remind them daily that they are special. Their lives have a purpose, even if they do not understand it. My goal is to transform their narratives, helping them see their value.

I am not a micromanager. I believe in empowering people to perform their duties without constant oversight. Micromanagement stifles creativity and motivation. Instead, I encourage my team to take ownership of their responsibilities, learn from their mistakes, and grow. If help is needed, I offer guidance, but I do not hover. This leadership approach encourages independence and innovation.

My background as a child of educators has taught me that learning is a lifelong process. If you do not know something, ask questions. No one has all the answers, but the willingness to seek knowledge differentiates successful people.

WORK-LIFE BALANCE, FAIRNESS, AND ETHICAL INTELLIGENCE

The concept of work-life balance is often misunderstood. Many organizations emphasize it, but by prioritizing work, they inadvertently prioritize labor over life. I reverse this: Life comes before work. Our personal lives have a direct impact on our professional performance. A stable home life leads to a more productive work life. Understanding this dynamic is crucial for fostering a healthy workplace. Balancing work and family was particularly challenging when my children were younger. All three boys played competitive soccer, and in the U.S., teams are structured by age groups. Each child was in a different league, requiring my wife and I to be in multiple places simultaneously. We had to travel to three other states some weekends for their games. We would divide and conquer, with my wife taking one child while I took another, and sometimes relying on trusted parents to help transport the third.

To ease this challenge, I arranged for them to play in the same age group, even if my youngest had to compete with older players. It was tough, but it shaped them into resilient athletes. I recall a moment when my youngest, Elliott, played so well that an opposing parent questioned his age, demanding to see his birth certificate. The assumption that he was older simply because of his skill level was frustrating and amusing. I stood my ground, ensuring they understood that my son belonged on that field just as much as any other player.

When my sons played varsity soccer in high school, there was a season when all three were simultaneously on the field. Seeing them play together was a proud moment, a testament to the sacrifices we made as parents to support their dreams. We spent countless weekends traveling, often staying in motels, navigating schedules, and ensuring they had everything they needed. It was not easy, but the lessons they learned from discipline, teamwork, and perseverance were invaluable.

Family always comes first. No matter how demanding my work may be, my responsibilities as a husband and father take precedence over it. Jobs come and go, but family is permanent. I ensure that I take vacations and spend quality time with my loved ones. Too often, people become consumed by work and regret not investing in their families. I refuse to make that mistake.

I firmly believe in the principles of procedural fairness and ethical intelligence. People are gifted with talents, but we are all different. If we can harmonize our strengths, the world will be a better place. Moral intelligence is the ability to distinguish right from wrong and act accordingly. Some individuals possess it naturally, while others struggle to develop it. It does not require formal education; it is an intrinsic quality that stems from a moral upbringing and values.

Fairness is not about rigid adherence to rules but about justice in execution. If I know that treating people with respect fosters mutual appreciation, why would I choose any other approach? Unfortunately, selfishness and greed corrupt workplaces and relationships. My role as a leader is to counteract these opposing forces by upholding fairness, transparency, and integrity.

NAVIGATING DIFFERENT CULTURAL WORK ENVIRONMENTS

Having worked in Nigeria, Ukraine, Spain, and the United States, I have experienced vastly different work cultures. In America, the first question people ask is, "What do you do?" In Europe, relationships are prioritized over titles. Before discussing professional roles, conversations revolve around family, background, and personal interests. Nigeria shares this relational approach, valuing connections over credentials.

However, I have noticed a shift in corporate America. Companies are now incorporating personal well-being into workplace culture, understanding that employees perform better when their personal lives are acknowledged. As a leader, I prioritize getting to know my team beyond their job descriptions. I learn their children's names, celebrate their milestones, and ensure they feel valued.

My philosophy is simple: treat people the way they want to be treated, with dignity and fairness. The world would be far better if more people adhered to this principle. Balancing personal and professional responsibilities requires authenticity. I lead at work the same way I do at home and in my nonprofit, and my children have seen this consistency throughout their lives. Initially, they struggled with my commitment to the orphanage, wondering why I invested so much time and resources there. However, as they grew older, they came to understand.

One of my proudest moments was hearing my eldest son, Enrique, speak at an event celebrating my PhD. He said, *"I've always known my dad to be this man. What you see is what you get. He does not change, and he does not waver when it comes to serving humanity."* Those words affirmed that I had done my job as a father. Ultimately, life is about service. Success is not measured by titles or wealth but by impact. I have truly lived if I can leave the world better than I found it.

MY MAJOR ACHIEVEMENTS AND LEGACY I PRAY TO LEAVE BEHIND

Career milestones and notable recognitions have shaped my journey in ways I never imagined. Growing up in Africa, I had dreams and aspirations, but I also understood that achieving them would require discipline, perseverance, and hard work. However, I have come to realize that success is mainly due to diligence, opportunity, and being prepared to meet them. No matter how prepared a person may be, without the right opportunities, their potential remains untapped.

One of my most outstanding career achievements was rising to the position of Vice President in a major corporation in the United States. This was something I never envisioned as a child. It was not because I was the most qualified or intelligent, but because I was consistent, diligent, and always exceeded expectations. I understood early on that being in the right place at the right time, combined with a strong work ethic, could open doors I never imagined.

Sitting in corporate boardrooms with top executives who made multi-billion-dollar decisions gave me firsthand insight into leadership, management, and global business strategy. I witnessed power, influence, and decision-making dynamics at the highest level. More importantly, I learned about how people operate under pressure, how leadership choices shape lives, and how values, or the lack thereof, influence an organization's culture.

Beyond my corporate career, my commitment to community development and social impact has led to numerous awards and recognitions. I have been honored for my work with Cornerstone of Hope Orphanage, receiving corporate and humanitarian awards that reaffirm that my efforts are making a difference. However, I do not measure my success by these accolades but by the number of lives I have touched and transformed.

The founding of Cornerstone of Hope Orphanage is undoubtedly one of my greatest life achievements. When I first envisioned starting an orphanage, I thought it would be small. I believed that if I were blessed with the means to care for one child, I would help one; if I could support two, I would take in two. But God had a much bigger plan.

Today, 151 children have gone through Cornerstone of Hope Orphanage. They have received shelter, education, healthcare, love, and an opportunity for a brighter future.

The name Cornerstone was intentionally chosen, inspired by Matthew 21:42, which speaks of the rejected stone becoming the cornerstone. Our orphanage embodies this ideal: it takes children who have been abandoned, forgotten, and overlooked by society, transforms their lives, and provides them with the foundation to succeed. At Cornerstone, we are not just providing charity; we are building lives. These children are not merely housed and fed; they are educated, mentored, and equipped to take their place in society. They are future doctors, engineers, teachers, and leaders.

Another significant way Cornerstone has impacted the community is by creating jobs. We employ caregivers, teachers, and administrative staff, each of whom contributes to their family's well-being through their wages. This cycle of economic empowerment is an extension of our mission to uplift communities.

Beyond employment, Cornerstone has also provided free water to the surrounding community. Many families in the area lack access to clean water, so our orphanage became a source of relief. However, this generosity was met with resistance when a local woman who sold water felt that our free supply was affecting her business. To prevent potential conflict and maintain peace in the community, our board made the painful decision to discontinue the free water program.

Still, our mission remains the same: *to serve, uplift, and transform lives.* The impact of Cornerstone of Hope Orphanage extends far beyond its walls. Of the one hundred fifty-one children who have passed through our care, nineteen, including my own adopted daughter, have been placed in loving homes in the United States. Seeing these children transition from despair to hope is one of the greatest joys of my life.

One of our biggest success stories is that of Patrick, a young man who left the orphanage system and pursued higher education in Leicester, United Kingdom. He studied accounting and returned to Nigeria, where he is now an entrepreneur. He runs a poultry farm that provides employment and food security for his community. His journey demonstrates that Cornerstone offers temporary relief and fosters sustainable change.

However, my extended family did not always understand my commitment to giving back. Many relatives questioned why I would invest so much time, energy, and resources in helping children I did not know. They believed that I should prioritize assisting family members instead. I have had to defend my decision multiple times, explaining that true generosity is not only about helping those related to you, but also about helping those who need it most.

Over time, some of these relatives have come to appreciate and even adopt this philosophy. Some have started giving back in their way, realizing that we all rise together by lifting others. The legacy of generosity does not end with me.

Philanthropy is contagious; when children grow up witnessing selflessness and kindness, they are more likely to carry those values forward. I may not be alive to see the full impact of what Cornerstone has set in motion, but I have faith that many of the children we have helped will pay it forward.

Looking to the future, my dream is expansion, not just in numbers but in impact. I want Cornerstone of Hope Orphanage to become a replicable model, bringing hope to more needy children. However, I recognize the importance of sustainability. Growth must be strategic and well-planned, ensuring we never compromise quality for quantity.

We continue to face challenges, including limited funding, government bureaucracy, and societal misconceptions about orphans. Many in Nigeria still stigmatize orphans, believing them to be cursed or unlucky. Some people assume that helping orphans brings misfortune, while others view orphanages with suspicion, fearing corruption or ulterior motives. These deep-seated societal beliefs cannot be changed overnight. However, even small shifts in perception are victories.

Change begins with action. I aim to inspire others through words and a consistent, visible, and meaningful impact. If I can change the mindset of even a handful of people, encouraging them to see orphans not as burdens but as future leaders, then my mission will be a success. Ultimately, the most significant achievement is not a title, an award, or a personal accomplishment; it is the lives that have been changed.

If I leave behind a legacy of love, service, and transformation, then I will have truly lived.

HOW ADVERSITY SHAPED ME

Life is a series of challenges and triumphs, and every test of character, faith, and belief has shaped and sculpted who we are today. My life, however, was not one of privilege and ease but of personal and professional struggle, one that instilled the lessons of tenacity, patience, and perseverance. Throughout childhood, life was not stable. I had dreams and aspirations early on, but my circumstances made achieving them impossible. In Nigeria, planning for the future was often an exercise in wishful thinking. You could set a ten-year goal, but circumstances could change so drastically that even a five-year plan seemed unrealistic. Survival was the immediate focus, and long-term aspirations often took a back seat to daily necessities.

Unlike those who inherited wealth or privilege, I had to build everything from the ground up. I did not come from a family of business moguls or professionals who could guide me in accumulating wealth or navigating the corporate world. Every step I took was a result of trial and error. This meant making difficult decisions about money, balancing the need to support my immediate and extended family, and ensuring the orphanage I had founded would remain thriving.

Sometimes, I made costly sacrifices, prioritizing the orphanage over personal comforts. There were moments when my family had to go without certain luxuries because I felt compelled to redirect resources to the children who had no one to care for them. My wife and children were incredibly understanding, but I knew they sometimes wished I had put them first.

Managing this emotional and financial burden created a significant amount of stress. The guilt of having a group of children depending on me, my relatives looking up to me, and my family at home having needs that, at times, were being put on the back burner was too much to bear. It was even affecting my health, raising my blood pressure and leaving me physically and mentally exhausted.

Aside from these challenges, the task of running the orphanage was a continuous one. There was never a moment when I could entirely switch off. My phone would ring at 2 a.m. Central Standard Time because of an emergency at the orphanage in Nigeria. A child was sick. A newborn had just been abandoned and brought to us by the officials of the Ministry, and now needed a name. Supplies were running low. Every crisis required my immediate attention, even if I was halfway across the world in the United States.

My professional journey was equally challenging. I did

not grow up with role models in the corporate world who could teach me how to navigate office politics, career growth, or leadership dynamics. I had to learn everything through experience and trial and error. My professional growth was fostered through workshops, training sessions, and the guidance of mentors I met along the way.

One of my biggest struggles in the workplace was learning how to navigate office culture and policies. I value honesty and direct communication, so I speak candidly when a company asks for staff meeting input. However, I quickly learned that honesty was not always welcomed. I was labeled as too loud or aggressive when I expressed my opinions. I was called too passive or uninterested when I chose to remain silent. No matter what I did, it felt like there was always a script I was expected to follow, one that I had not been given.

There were also more insidious challenges, like racial bias and discrimination. Despite my education, training, and strong work ethic, I found that some doors were closed to me, and less qualified individuals were able to move ahead. When I complained of these discriminatory practices, I was branded "difficult" or "not a team player." It was disheartening and frustrating to watch less experienced people being assigned leadership responsibilities that I could perform simply because of prejudices that had nothing to do with their ability. Nevertheless, despite these frustrations, I learned valuable lessons that molded my character and determination.

Patience strengthened me. Some battles are worth fighting, while others are best left to silence. I learned to observe more and speak less. I discovered that sometimes, the best way to change a system is not to challenge it head-on but to work around it, creating impact in quieter but more meaningful ways.

I also learned the importance of emotional endurance. Some situations in life are unfair, but reacting emotionally or with frustration rarely brings about change. Instead, I channeled my experiences into something more significant: mentoring younger professionals, advocating for those who faced similar struggles, and using my influence to create opportunities for others.

One of my greatest resilience teachers has been the children from the orphanage. Despite having so little, they smile, laugh, and delight in the simplest pleasures. Being around them makes me realize that resilience isn't so much about holding on during adversity as it is about holding on to hope in the face of hopelessness.

My children have also taught me a thing or two. American kids are outspoken. They challenge authority, ask questions, and stand up for their beliefs. In Nigeria, where I was raised, it was unheard of to question authority. You obeyed, like it or not, no questions asked. However, seeing my children question others and express their views assertively led me to appreciate the virtue of standing up for one's convictions.

Over time, I have learned to choose my battles wisely. There are still days when I look back and wish I had spoken up more. Yet, I have also come to value the understanding that not every battle must be fought immediately. Some battles are won by waiting, timing your moment, and acting strategically instead of reacting.

Faith has also been a significant part of my resiliency. I have learned that not everyone who claims to be Christ-like acts like Him. Many of the same individuals who practice discrimination in the workplace or ignore injustices in society sit in church pews every Sunday. This realization compelled me to distinguish between genuine faith and performative religion.

I have learned to trust God's justice rather than man's judgment. Resilience doesn't just mean getting through difficulty but also learning through it. Every test and trial has toughened, humbled, and made me more determined to leave the world a better place when I leave it.

The struggles that I have faced hardened me to the point of becoming a being who will always emerge victorious. I have suffered poverty, experienced the death of a loved one, and experienced discrimination and rejection. Doors have shut on me, judged, and misunderstood.

I have also built a purpose-driven life, transformed the

lives of hundreds of children, and worked to create a legacy of untold worth. Throughout it all, I clung to the belief that setbacks are not failures but foreshadowings of even greater triumphant successes. As long as I continue to grow, learn, and serve, I know that all the adversity I have ever experienced was worth it.

MY REFLECTION ON TURNING 60

Reaching the milestone of 60 years old is both humbling and surreal. It feels as though time has moved too quickly, slipping through my fingers before I could fully grasp it. There was a time when I had boundless energy, could rise early, accomplish everything on my to-do list, and still have time left for more. Now, I pause, reflect, and ask, *"How did I get here so fast?"*

When I was younger, I had grand visions of my life. I once thought I would retire at 35, but that never happened. I believed I would have accomplished all my dreams by age 50, but that was an illusion. Life has its plans. Aging has taught me that while dreams and goals are essential, the real journey lies in the experiences they bring.

Aging is a reality that no one can fully grasp until they begin to feel it. As a young African boy, I lived one day at a time. Tomorrow felt distant, almost unreachable, especially when life was complicated. Some days, I longed for time to pass more quickly, so I could escape hardships and hope the next day would be different. But now, I look back and realize how quickly those days turned into years and how those years brought me to this very moment.

THE REALITY OF LOSS AND THE GIFT OF TIME

One of the most defining experiences in my life was losing my two younger brothers, Mr. Ekenuhunrie Idehen and Dr. Nelson Idehen. Losing not just one but two accomplished adults within a six-month period changed me forever. It altered my perception of life, priorities, and the concept of time itself.

It reminded me of how fleeting life can be, how uncertain tomorrow is, and how important it is to focus on what truly matters. These losses made me wiser, and my faith in God strengthened. I stopped questioning Him in the ways I used to. Instead of asking, *"Why did this happen?"* I started asking, *"What can I learn from this?"*

Looking back, I see that many of my childhood dreams have become a reality. As a young boy, I always wished to go to America. I am here today. I used to long for jeans and tennis shoes, things I couldn't afford when I was growing up. Now, I own them, but I hardly even notice them. I once admired people who drove Mercedes-Benz cars, thinking owning one would be the peak of success. But when I finally got one, I realized it was just a means of transportation. The things that once felt unattainable have now become ordinary.

Aging has taught me that the things we once desperately chased may not hold the meaning we expect once we attain them. It is not about material possessions, titles, or status. It is about impact. It is about the legacy we leave behind.

WITNESSING GENERATIONS GROW

One of the most rewarding moments of my life happened in 2024 in Greensboro, North Carolina, when I attended the wedding of a young woman who had once been a child in an orphanage. She was adopted in 2007 and brought to the United States, and now, she was walking down the aisle as a bride. Seeing her start her own family, knowing she once had no one and was now surrounded by love, was a moment of profound fulfillment.

Even more remarkable was that my son and daughter were able to witness it with me. That day, I was reminded that *hope is alive*. People often struggle to believe in hope because they do not see the circumstances that lead to its fulfillment. They pray, wish, wait, and give up when things don't happen immediately. But I have learned that just because something hasn't happened yet doesn't mean it won't. Some dreams take time, and some prayers are answered in unexpected ways.

I once prayed to go to the United States, and I got there. I prayed for a family, and now I have one. I prayed to help one child, and today, we have helped over 150 children at the orphanage. Not everything I wanted happened. I wanted to be a pilot, but that never came to pass. But I understand now that some things are not meant to be, which is okay.

LIFE'S LESSONS IN PATIENCE AND PERSPECTIVE

One of the greatest lessons I have learned on my journey to 60 is the importance of patience. When we pray for something that doesn't happen immediately, we assume the answer is no, but sometimes the answer is *not yet*. Other times, the answer is never, but only because something better awaits us.

In my younger years, I complained a lot. In Ukraine, I grumbled about the cold weather and the complex language. When I went to Spain, I grumbled about having to learn Spanish. Today, however, the same experiences that I complained about have benefited me on my journey. The languages I was made to learn have aided me in a way I could not have imagined.

Whenever I encounter problems, I remind myself that they could always be worse. I think of the children at the orphanage who have experienced the worst and always have a smile on their faces. If they, having so little, can smile so readily, then why am I complaining?

LOOKING AHEAD

As I grow older, my body reminds me that I am not as strong as I used to be. The back and knee pain are signs that I have put a lot of mileage on this body. The grey hairs have taken over, and while people tell me I still look good, I know I am not the man I was 20 years ago. What I pray for now is *good health*. I would choose good health over riches any day. With good health, I can continue serving, caring for more children, and fulfilling my purpose.

I dream of Cornerstone of Hope Orphanage becoming a beacon of hope for Nigeria and the world. I hope that the children we have raised will go on to share love, build hope, and change lives. I hope they will become responsible individuals who will go out into the world and do for others what was once done for them.

One day, there may be no more orphans on the streets, and every child will have a home. I may not live to see that day, but if the number of abandoned children continues to decrease, I will know that we have made a difference.

UNDERSTANDING THE NATURE OF DREAMS

One of the hardest lessons I have learned is that *your dream is your dream*, and no one else will fully understand it. People will offer to help, but they will never share your passion for your dream. Some will walk with you, but eventually slow down, questioning whether you are doing too much. Some will even try to change your dream, convincing you to scale back, settle, or stop.

I have had people tell me that I am wasting my time. They say I should have used the resources for my extended family instead of taking care of strangers, and that I should not have sent Patrick to the UK for education when I could have sent my relative's child instead. It was then that I realized that people will always prioritize their interests. And that is okay. Psychology teaches that human behavior is not easily changed but only influenced. I cannot force people to see the world through my eyes. I can only continue living my truth, hoping that some will be inspired to do the same.

THE LEGACY I WANT TO LEAVE BEHIND

When my time on earth is done, I do not wish to be remembered for the job titles I held, the degrees I earned, or the accolades that once adorned my résumé. Those things, while honorable in their own right, are fleeting. They do not define the core of who I am or the purpose for which I live. I want to be remembered as the man who saw—and acted—the man who didn't just walk past brokenness or close his eyes to the suffering of others. I want people to say, *"He showed up. Not with empty words or promises, but with hands ready to serve and a heart wide open."*

Let my legacy be written in the laughter of children who once had no home but found shelter, safety, and love because I chose to care. Let it echo in the stories of families who were fed when they had nothing, and in the quiet prayers of those whose hope was restored by a simple gesture of kindness. I want to be known not as someone who sought recognition, but as someone who heard God's call and responded in obedience. Not out of obligation. Not for applause. But because it was the right thing to do. Because compassion demanded a response. Because faith without action is empty.

Ultimately, we are not measured by the wealth we accumulate or the success the world celebrates. We are measured by the love we give, the burdens we help carry, and the lives we leave better than we found them. I want people to say that I lived fully, gave generously, forgave freely, and loved deeply. That I walked with integrity, served with humility, and believed fiercely in the good that could come from even the smallest act of hope. That is the legacy I want to leave behind.

AFTERWORD

My Message to Readers

As I close this book, I want to leave you with one thing: *hope*. Hope isn't some theoretical romanticism or mere optimism but a living, pulsating power that will carry you through the worst moments of your life. When informed by faith and an awareness of a transcendent purpose, hope can bridge the gap between despair and purpose, struggle and triumph.

No matter where you are or how uncertain the road ahead may seem, I want you to know that there is always light at the end of the tunnel. You may not see it yet, and feel lost in the darkness. But if you hold on and keep moving forward, you will one day look back and realize that the light was there all along, sometimes flickering, sometimes hidden behind obstacles, but never truly gone.

Life is full of tunnels: periods of hardship, uncertainty, and pain. Some are short, some seem endless, and some are so dark that we wonder if we will ever emerge. However, the beauty of a tunnel lies in its impermanence. It is a passage, a transition from one place to another. You will emerge victorious if you keep walking and believing.

I know this because I have experienced it firsthand. I have faced moments when I thought I had nothing left, when I questioned my purpose, faith, and ability to keep going. I have known what it feels like to lose loved ones, face setbacks, give and not receive, pour my heart into something, and wonder if it was all in vain. But every time I reached what felt like the end, something small, sometimes miraculous, would remind me to keep going.

Hope is not always about expecting the best-case scenario, where everything works out; it's about realizing that something is stirring, even when it's quiet, and none of it makes sense. Sometimes, the most significant steps forward happen in silence. Sometimes, the biggest acts of hope aren't the big, heroic acts but the everyday, ordinary moments of grace: a kind word, a quiet prayer, a stranger's generosity, the resilience in your own heart that refuses to give up.

If you take anything from this book, I hope it is this: ***Your story is not over. You were created for a reason and are here for a purpose. None of the struggles you have faced, the battles you have fought, or the victories you have won are wasted. Every trial, every tribulation, and every celebration is part of a bigger picture. Maybe you can't observe it now, but one day you will.***

MY FINAL REFLECTION

Looking back, it is evident that every setback, every triumph, and every unexpected detour led to the development of the person in front of you today. I did not come alone. I am the result of the sacrifices, prayers, and devotion of the people who have lived before me. I am here because of the kindness of strangers, the guidance of mentors, and the unshakable grace of God. And that is why I give. That is why I serve. Because I know what it feels like to need a helping hand, to be on the edge of despair, and to find hope in the kindness of others. I know what it means to be given a second chance, to have someone believe in you when you have stopped believing in yourself. Now, I want to be that person for others.

Once you've dropped this book, passed it along, or placed it on your bookshelf, remember these few things, hold on to them, and never let go. Let these words remind you always to choose your own path, led by God and anchored in His word.

- *Pray to leave behind a legacy of love, service, and a life lived in faith.*
- *Be not remembered by the possessions you had, but by the gifts you gave.*
- *Don't get remembered by the jobs you had, but by the people you have touched.*
- *Not for the wealth you have gained but for the hope you*

have given.

- *May your life serve as a living testimony of the power of faith, resilience, and compassion.*

I want you to know that you have the power to do the same and even greater work. Your call and purpose may not be the same as mine. Yours may be in the quietness of your home, raising your children, maybe serving in your community or the church. No matter what you've been called to, you can transform lives. You can change lives no matter where you come from or what your struggles are. It doesn't take millions of dollars or grand gestures; it starts with a willingness to love, serve, and see the humanity in others.

Love without limits. Give without expectations. Believe without ceasing. No matter what life throws your way or how many times you stumble, *rise again. Keep walking. Keep believing. Keep holding on to hope.* One day, when you look back, you will see that you were never alone; hope was with you all along, guiding you toward the light.

Appendix

Over the years, I have been fortunate to receive numerous awards and recognitions for my contributions to my professional field and humanitarian work. While I do not serve for accolades, these acknowledgments remind me that my work makes a tangible difference. I also hope they inspire you to pursue your dreams, build capacity, join a community, and, above all, make a difference.

This appendix records the journey that has shaped my life and mission. While dates and accolades are milestones, the real story is in the impact, the lives touched, and the lessons learned. This is not just a timeline but a testament to faith, perseverance, and the boundless power of love. Though appreciated, these awards are not an accurate measure of success. The greatest reward is seeing lives transformed through love, education, and opportunity.

AWARDS, RECOGNITIONS, AND PROFESSIONAL ACHIEVEMENTS:

- Numerous awards from Wells Fargo, including: **2001** Wells Fargo Star Teller Award, **2003** Wells Fargo Service

Award, **2003** Wells Fargo Online Star Award, **2003, 2005, 2007, 2008 & 2009** Wells Fargo Diversity Champion Awards, **2005** Sales & Service Medal, **2006** Central Iowa Diversity Recognition Award, **2007** Volunteer Leave Program and Volunteer Service Excellence Award (National). **2016** Volunteer Service Award (National).

- **2006-** Named an Influential Business & Civic leader in Des Moines, Iowa.
- **2007-** Community Commitment Award from the African American Leadership Coalition.
- **2007-** Iowa Council for International Understanding (ICIU) Community Leadership Award.
- **2007-** Int. Trends and Services Award from the Des Moines Chapter of Links, Inc.
- **2008-** Member of the Iowa Council for International Understanding, recognized for his volunteer work with immigrants settling in Iowa.
- **2008-** Heroes of the Heartland–International Impact Award from the American Red Cross.
- **2009-** Business Fellows to the Middle East–Dubai & Egypt. Went to Dubai and Egypt as part of a Business for Diplomatic Action program. Worked with local government leaders, business groups, Non-Governmental Organizations, nonprofits, and media companies to identify how American businesses can best work with

Middle Eastern companies.
- **2009-** Dr. David J Wang Humanitarian Award from the Chinese Association of Iowa.
- Honored as the **2009** recipient of the Dr. David Jiagian Wang Award for Humanity.
- **2009-** Graduated from the first FBI Citizens' Academy in the state of Iowa
- **2010-** Director's Community Leadership Awards.
- **2010-** Federal Bureau of Investigation Director's Community Leadership National Award.
- **2019-** Iowa Chinese Achievement Award for Outstanding Achievement Award for Advising on Youth, Professional, Social, Cultural, and Business Development
- **2020-** Community Development Director at AmeriFirst Financial Corporation
- **2024** – Transitioned to nonprofit leadership at DMACC's Evelyn K. Davis (EKD) Center in Des Moines for Working Families, merging business acumen with philanthropy.
- Served as the President and CEO at OPX International LLC, Community Development Director at AmeriFirst Financial Corporation
- Board of the local Iowa Red Cross,
- An active member of the Alianza-Latino Business Association

- An active member of the Iowa Chinese Association
- Creation of the Citizens' Academy Alumni Association for the Omaha Division, serving on the executive board.
- Vice President, Community Development Officer at Wells Fargo Bank, N.A.
- United Way Des Moines OpportUNITY Council
- CultureALL Ambassador
- Executive Leader- International Business S&T Consulting Ltd
- Appeared on PBS American Portrait
- Board Member, Northwest Rotary Club
- Past board and Committee membership, Iowa Community Capitol,
- Past board and Committee membership, 6th Avenue Corridor
- Past board and Committee membership, OneEconomy
- Past board and Committee membership: Iowa Literacy Council,
- Board Member of Central Iowa
- The New Iowan Centers Community Advisory Committee
- The Greater Des Moines Partnership Diversity Committee,
- Board Member Iowa International Center, etc.
- Unit Director for the Ellis Levitt Boys and Girls Clubs

in Des Moines, Iowa
- Board member, ICIU
- Board member, Links Leadership Institute
- Board member, Wells Fargo Mountain Midwest Region Diversity Council
- Board member, The New Iowans Policy Task Force
- Board member, Refugee Cooperative Service Board
- Board member, Employer Support of Guards and Reserve (ESGR)
- Board member, Lutheran Church of Hope Council

VOLUNTEER EXPERIENCE
- **2005 -** Present Founder and Chief Executive Officer for Cornerstone of Hope Inc.
- **2007-2009:** Board member of the Political and Economic Research Council (PERC).
- **2007 - 2011** Member/Board of the Des Moines Rotary International Club.
- **2010 - 2014** Grand View University Diversity Committee (member).
- African National Association of Iowa (**member September 2015 - Present**)
- Iowa Community Capital board (**member June 2016 - Present**)
- Greater Des Moines Supportive Housing Board (**June**

2016 – July 2017).
- FBI Citizen Academy Alumni Association Board **(member May 2011 – May 2017),**
- **2018 - 2020** Member/Board of the Northwest Rotary International Club.
- Genesis Incorporated (Advisory Board member)
- 6th Avenue Corridor Board (member)
- Greater Des Moines Partnership Equity and Inclusion Committee **(member 2017 - Present).**
- One Economy Board **(member 2018 - 2020)**
- Iowa Literacy Council board **(member/VP January 2018 - 2020)**
- Board member, Greater Des Moines Partnership Diversity Committee.
- Designed a philanthropic giving program aligned with strategic priorities, achieved 'outstanding' ratings in regulatory exams, and positioned Wells Fargo as a notable company in diverse communities.

TIMELINE OF KEY EVENTS IN MY LIFE

A chronological overview of significant moments in my personal, professional, and philanthropic journey:

EARLY LIFE & EDUCATION:
- **1965-** Born in Ekehuan, Nigeria, into a humble family

with strong values in education and resilience.
- **1971-1977:** attended Edaiken Primary School, where I first developed an interest in Arithmetic.
- **1977-** Enrolled in Edo Boys High School, now called Adolor College, Benin City, excelling in science subjects.
- **1983-** Gained admission into Federal Auchi Polytechnic in Auchi, Nigeria, and earned a Higher National Diploma in Quantity Surveying.
- **1986-** Earned a first degree -National Diploma in Quantity Surveying, shaping my career path.
- **1986-** Secured my first job at VITA Construction Ltd., Lagos, Nigeria, where I learned responsibility, integrity, hard work, and accountability.
- **1993-** Moved to Ukraine to pursue higher education and expand opportunities.
- **1997-** Moved to Spain in search of a better life.
- **1997 –** Got Married.
- **1999 –** Had our first son.
- **2000 –** Had our second son.
- **2000 –** Moved to the United States.
- **2001 –** Had our third son.
- **2005-** Became a **Vice President** at Wells Fargo Bank, overseeing Community Development for the State of Iowa.
- **2014-** Earned a Master of Business Administration

(MBA) degree from the University of Phoenix
- **2018-** Earned a Master of Philosophy
- **2023-** Doctor of Philosophy (Ph.D.) in Industrial and Organizational Psychology from Walden University.

PHILANTHROPY & HUMANITARIAN WORK:

- **2005-** Founded **Cornerstone of Hope Orphanage**, fulfilling a lifelong promise to God.
- **2007-** Witnessed the adoption of the first child from Cornerstone, a milestone for the orphanage.
- **2008-** Expanded the orphanage to accommodate more children and provide sustainable resources.
- **2024-** Hosted the first wedding of a former orphan from **Cornerstone**, a moment of deep fulfillment.

REFLECTIONS & MILESTONES:

- **May 3, 2025–** Published and launched 2 Books: *Born to Serve and Bridging Expectations.* Sharing my journey with the world to inspire future generations.
- **May 19, 2025–** Turn 60
- **July 26, 2025-** celebrates turning 60, reflecting on decades of service, leadership, and purpose.

Excerpts from Speeches and Writings

Below are quotes from speeches and personal writings that encapsulate my philosophy on life, leadership, and giving back.

On Leadership & Purpose:
"True leadership is not about being in charge but taking responsibility. It is about serving without expectation, lifting others, and creating a legacy of love that outlives you."

On Faith & Resilience:
"I have walked through many storms in life, but I have never walked alone. Every challenge and trial has been a reminder that even in the darkness, God's grace is sufficient."

On Giving & Legacy:
"I do not measure success by the wealth I accumulate, but by the number of lives I impact. If I can leave behind a generation of children who know love, who know hope, and

who know they are valued, then I have lived well."

On Hope:

"Hope is not passive. It is a force that drives us forward, even when the road is uncertain. It is the whisper in our hearts that says, 'Keep going, your story is not over yet.'"

Dr. Eric Edokpaigbe Idehen

Dr. Eric Edokpaigbe Idehen

www.ingramcontent.com/pod-product-compliance
Lightning Source LLC
Chambersburg PA
CBHW061759070526
44586CB00023B/2638